GOOD NEWS FOR THE HARD OF HEARING

Sermons For
Pentecost (Middle Third)
Cycle A, Gospel Texts

ROGER G. TALBOTT

Roger D. Talbott

CSS Publishing Company, Inc.
Lima, Ohio

GOOD NEWS FOR THE HARD OF HEARING

Library of Congress Cataloging-in-Publication Data

Talbott, Roger G., 1948-
    Good News for the hard of hearing : sermons for Pentecost (middle third) : Cycle A Gospel lesson texts / Roger G. Talbott.
        p. cm.
    Includes bibliographical references.
    ISBN 0-7880-0506-5
    1. Pentecost season — Sermons. 2. Bible N.T. Gospels — Sermons. 3. Sermons, En-glish. I. Title.
 BV61.T35   1995
252'.67—dc20   95-14046
                                                                                  CIP

This book is available in the following formats, listed by ISBN:
0-7880-0506-5 Book
0-7880-0507-3 IBM 3 1/2 computer disk
0-7880-0508-1 IBM 3 1/2 book and disk package
0-7880-0509-X Macintosh computer disk
0-7880-0510-3 Macintosh book and disk package
0-7880-0511-1 IBM 5 1/4 computer disk
0-7880-0512-X IBM 5 1/4 book and disk package

PRINTED IN U.S.A

This is dedicated to
the people of North Olmsted United Methodist Church
who listen to me,
and to
Jacquie, Matt, and Jim
who love me.

Editor's Note Regarding The Lectionary

During the past two decades there has been an attempt to move in the direction of a uniform lectionary among various Protestant denominations.

•Lectionary Uniformity

Preaching on the same scripture lessons every Sunday is a step in the right direction of uniting Christians of many faiths. If we are reading the same scriptures together we may also begin to accomplish other achievements. Our efforts will be strengthened through our unity.

•Christian Unity

Beginning with Advent 1995 The Evangelical Lutheran Church in America will drop its own lectionary schedule and adopt the Revised Common Lectionary.

•ELCA Adopts Revised Common Lectionary

We at CSS Publishing Company heartily embrace this change. We recognize, however, that there will be a transitional period during which some churches may continue for a time to use the traditional Lutheran lectionary. In order to accommodate these clergy and churches who may still be referring to the Lutheran lectionary we will for a period of time continue to provide sermons and illustrations based on scriptural passages from BOTH the Lutheran and The Revised Common lectionaries.

•For Those In Transition

Table Of Contents

C — Revised Common Lectionary; L — Lutheran Lectionary; RC — Roman Catholic Lectionary

Preface

When his disciples asked Jesus why he always spoke in parables, Jesus answered that it was because "this people's heart has grown dull, and their ears are hard of hearing ..." (Matthew 13:15). One of the themes of Matthew's gospel is how little even the disciples heard although they were the ones to whom were revealed the secrets of the kingdom.

I wear a hearing aid in each ear, so I know something about communicating with the hard of hearing. Being hearing-impaired is not the same as being nearsighted. Amplification alone does not make me able to hear in the same way that my glasses make me able to see. I am not different from people with normal hearing. I hear best what I want to hear and I shut out the things I don't want to hear. I hear, "Great sermon, Pastor!" better than I hear, "I notice your hair is getting thinner." I also hear best what I expect to hear. The conventional reply to my question, "How are you?" registers more quickly and more accurately than, "I just found out I have leukemia."

I have the same problem with the gospel. I have no problem at all hearing the good news that I am forgiven. I have a really hard time hearing a parable that tells me I will suffer the tortures of the damned until I forgive. And no matter how often I hear the story, I still expect those workers who started at sunrise to get paid more than the ones who only worked for an hour.

People get through to me by making me want to hear. I want to hear stories. I want to hear humor. I want to hear things that make my life meaningful, solve my problems, overcome my fears. When all else fails, repetition gets the message across.

These sermons have been influenced by preachers who have gotten through to me despite my spiritual hearing impairment. Craddock, Buechner and Lowry have taught me the importance of imagination and narrative. David Buttrick showed me how to follow the "moves" of the scripture lesson. Harry Emerson Fosdick made me problem-centered. Two great preachers who never made the national stage also influenced me: Leonard Budd, now at

Cleveland's Church of the Savior (United Methodist), taught me how to paint a picture with words and Eugene Umberger, who taught Religion at Hartwick College before becoming pastor of one of the Presbyterian churches in Oneonta, showed me that it was possible to preach a meaningful, thoughtful sermon almost every Sunday and that one preacher could present the message of the gospel using a variety of styles.

The most important influences on these sermons never stood in a pulpit, however. These sermons are one side of a continuing dialogue with the people of North Olmsted United Methodist Church. Every sermon is an attempt to answer a question they are asking or to speak to some situation they are facing. To the extent that their questions and life-situations are universal, the sermons will have a universal appeal. To the extent that their questions and life-situations are unique, other preachers will have to make their own connections to their congregations. I am indebted to my mother who taught me how to read and to love the Bible and to my father who taught me how to tell a story and gave me his sense of humor. Above all, these sermons are influenced by the three most important people in my world. Matt and Jim share their mother's conviction that being honest is a lot more loving than being nice, whether one is preaching a sermon or critiquing it afterward. They demand both intellectual honesty and sincerity of presentation. Jacquie has listened to more of my sermons than anyone. She sat on a log while, as a teenager, I preached to campers at a local campground. She sat on the pews of a tiny rural church when I was in seminary and a giant urban church when I was an associate. She has taught me three things about preaching: it's a sin to be manipulative, think about how this sermon sounds to the outsider, and remember that there are a lot of things in life that are more important than next Sunday's sermon.

Professors Of Paradox

Once upon a time, a strange old man came to a small village. He carried a mixing bowl and a wooden spoon. This sight was odd enough to cause the people of the village to notice what the old man did next.

The old man took the bowl to the plowed field next to the village and he put some dirt into the bowl until it was about half full. Then he went to the village pump and filled it with water to about an inch below the brim. Then the old man sat down on a rock next to the pump and began to stir the water into the dirt with the wooden spoon. He stirred and stirred and stirred. The people watched this without much interest until the old man became visibly excited. He peered happily into the bowl and then reached in and pulled out a mud-covered pebble. He then went to the pump and washed it off and held it up in the sun to inspect it. The people came closer and they could see that it was a gold nugget.

The old man then went back to stirring. He stirred and stirred for a long time and then again he became excited, pulled something out of the bowl, washed it off and held another gold nugget in his hand. This went on for a long time: the old man stirring and stirring and every once in awhile, excitedly retrieving gold nuggets from the bowl.

11

Finally, when he had a half-dozen gold nuggets lined up next to him, the old man stopped stirring, washed out the bowl at the pump, picked up the nuggets and then went on his way.

As you can imagine, no sooner had the strange old man disappeared over the horizon than the people of the village seized their bowls and spoons, scooped some dirt into the bowls, filled them with water and began to stir. They stirred and stirred. Even though they stirred and stirred for hours and looked and looked and occasionally ran their fingers through the mud in the bowl, no gold nuggets appeared. Many of them began to tire of this. The rich put down their bowls because they already had enough gold. The children put down their bowls because playing was more important to them than gold nuggets. The young men and women put down their bowls because love was much more important to them than gold nuggets. The poor kept on stirring the longest, but most of them finally gave up, deciding that there were better ways to feed themselves and their families.

At last, only one poor woman was left. She kept stirring until it became too dark to see and then she resumed the task the next morning and stirred all day again with no results, but she kept on stirring. Finally, as evening was falling again, the poor woman saw the strange old man returning.

The old man came to the spot where the poor woman was stirring and stirring the mud in the bowl and asked what she was doing.

The poor woman explained that she had seen the old man stir mud the day before and pull out gold nuggets. She wondered why she could not do the same.

The old man inspected the bowl, asked about the dirt and the water and scratched his head with puzzlement. "It is all the same," he said. "I don't know why it isn't working."

After a few more minutes of thought the old man said, "Oh, there *is* one more thing. When you are stirring the mud, you can't be thinking about gold nuggets."

To stir mud without thinking about gold nuggets is a paradox — like finding treasure in a field. The dictionary says that a paradox is a statement that seems to be contradictory or contrary to common sense, but which may be true. The parables in this passage are filled with paradoxes. On the one hand, Jesus says, the kingdom of heaven is like a treasure hidden in a field — something *we* must find and something we must be willing to give everything for. On the other hand, the kingdom of heaven is like a merchant looking for a rare pearl. In other words, the kingdom of heaven comes looking for *us*, and gives everything for our sake.

On the one hand, said Jesus, the kingdom of heaven is like a net that catches every kind of fish in the sea. The kingdom of heaven has the original policy of nondiscrimination. On the other hand, Jesus says, the kingdom of heaven will be like the angels sorting the fish. The good ones will be kept and the bad ones will be thrown away. In other words, the kingdom of heaven is highly discriminating — a very exclusive realm.

"Do you understand?" Jesus asks his disciples.

They say that they do.

Jesus says that his disciples must become professors of paradox. He uses the word *scribe*. The scribes were the professors, the learned people, the teachers and interpreters of the word of God. Professors of paradox can handle contradictions. They are able to see the value in both the old and the new. They can stir the mud and not think of gold nuggets. We have to be professors of paradox in order to grasp what Jesus is saying about the kingdom of heaven in these parables.

The first thing that Jesus says about the kingdom is that it is something we must find, yet we discover it accidentally. The poet, Robert Frost, once wrote to his friend Sidney Cox, "Our minds are so crowded with what we have been told to look for that they have no room for accidental discoveries." [1]

Most of the things really worth finding in life are accidental discoveries. Think about the way most people meet their future spouses. I know a young woman who turned around during the passing of the peace at her church and shook hands with a man sitting directly behind her. They were married 18 months later.

I know another story: A groom asked a friend to be his best man at his wedding and the best man spent the entire wedding reception with the maid of honor and in a year they were married.

Thirty years later the first groom lost his wife and two years later the maid of honor lost her husband. The widower sent the new widow a note of condolence. The widow wrote back her heartfelt thanks. They got together to share some memories and tears. They started to heal. Tears of grief gradually became tears of laughter and life began again for both of them surprisingly, unexpectedly.

"The kingdom of heaven is like treasure hidden in a field, which someone found and hid; then in his joy he goes and sells all that he has and buys that field."

"Do you understand?" Jesus asked his disciples. "Yes," they said, and we say "Yes," too. We do understand. We understand that the best things in life, the things we would give our very lives for, are discovered by accident.

I mean, it's an accident and it isn't an accident. The people who accidentally stumble upon someone they want to share their lives with, whether that person is a stranger or someone they have known all their lives, usually are people who are consciously or unconsciously looking for someone special.

The strange thing is that people who are looking too hard for a mate, who are too desperate or who have too clear an idea of exactly what they are looking for, are the least likely to find a treasure. Their neediness may drive other people away; or they may latch on to the first person who comes along, even though that person is entirely unsuited to them; or they may overlook the right person because he or she doesn't fit their preconceived notions of what their future spouse should be like.

Those who do find — the ones who seem to stumble on the real treasures — are often the ones who say, "Well, I had just decided that it probably wasn't going to happen to me," or "that was the last place I expected to meet anyone," or "the thing that surprised me the most was that she isn't my type at all."

The scribes of the kingdom have to be professors of paradox; people who can stir the bowl of mud but not think about finding gold nuggets. The nugget the ordinary scribes were looking for was a Messiah who looked like a king. The nugget a lot of people who came to Jesus were looking for was physical health. He gave it to them, but that wasn't the kingdom. Other people were looking for the gold nugget of peace of mind and Jesus drove out their demons, but that wasn't the treasure of the kingdom either. Others thought the gold nugget was acceptance and closeness to someone else, and Jesus gave them his friendship and welcomed them into his fellowship, and they were closer to the kingdom, but that wasn't the kingdom either.

What is this kingdom? This treasure?

Jesus never says what it is, exactly. We might translate the phrase as the government of God or the reign of God. Jesus sometimes calls it eternal life or abundant life, too. Jesus never says exactly what it is, but he does tell us it is like a treasure hidden in a field.

That part of the world where Jesus lived was (and is) a land swept by wars and invasions. Every time people heard that invaders were coming they would bury their valuables in spots that only they knew about. When the threat passed, they dug them up again.

Sometimes the invaders carried away the owner and the treasure stayed buried, forgotten. Generations may have come and gone, plowing the fields over the top of the treasure. For the treasure to be found again, two things had to happen. Frost and earth tremors had to push the treasure upward toward the surface and someone had to come along who was looking for treasure, but not looking for anything in particular. It had to be someone whose head was not so full of what he had been taught to look for that he could not discover anything accidentally. In other words, it had to be a professor of paradox: someone hungry enough, poor enough, desperate enough to keep stirring the mud in the bowl, yet without thinking about gold nuggets.

The people who find the treasure are not the ones who grow tired of looking and lose interest; nor the ones who are already satisfied with life; nor those who are so discouraged that they give up. Do you understand this? Of course you do.

When you are hungry, you see signs for food everywhere. When you are lonely, you look into your mailbox and if there is a personal letter there, you will see it even under all the junk mail and the bills! You don't know who could be writing. You didn't expect a letter really, but you saw it when it came. When you are poor, it's amazing how you can spot a nickel on the sidewalk and a bargain in a store window. When you are grieving, your ears seem to pick up comforting words or your eyes seem to fall upon comforting pictures, even though you couldn't imagine that anything could bring you comfort.

"Blessed are the poor."

"Blessed are those who mourn."

"Blessed are those who hunger and thirst."

Our search for the kingdom is prompted by a hunger that is deeper than our hunger for food and a loneliness that other people cannot fill. Our search is prompted by the grief we feel about our own deaths and a poverty that cannot be measured by the balance in our bank accounts.

We only have to be careful to keep our minds open to accidental discoveries. If our minds are full of things we have been taught to look for, like a particular kind of religious experience, or a particular kind of religious community, or a particular kind of emotional or psychological or physical cure, we won't find the kingdom.

We find the kingdom by being hungry and by being open to whatever will fill that hunger. It is also necessary for the treasure to come to the surface so that the seeker may find.

"Again, the kingdom of heaven is like a merchant in search of fine pearls; on finding one pearl of great value, he went and sold all that he had and bought it."

The kingdom of heaven comes looking for us like a merchant looking for pearls or like a shepherd looking for a lost sheep.

One of the things we find when we accidentally stumble on the kingdom is that the kingdom has been looking for us all the time — the king has been looking for us. That is one way of expressing what the treasure is — it is the discovery that we are *treasured*.

Carol Pearson recently said that "psychologists have a term for that rare disorder which they call 'delusions of grandeur,' but they have no term for the disorder common to nearly all of us — the delusion of insignificance and worthlessness." [2]

The treasure of the kingdom gives us a sense of worth that no job, no title, no human love, no skill or accomplishment could ever give us. I see this so often in people who have newly discovered the kingdom. They often talk as if the entire universe were set up for their convenience and encouragement and education. "God helped me find a job." "God must have told you to send me that letter. It was just what I needed at exactly the right moment." "God gave me cancer to teach me to be more compassionate." I used to be turned off by this kind of talk, and I still am if it isn't sincere. Often it is sincere. People who talk like this really believe that God cares at least as much about them as God does about the lilies of the field and the birds of the air. They believe that everything works for good for those who love God and are called according to God's purposes. Somehow they come to believe that they were foreordained, predestined, if you will, to be plowing in that field the day the treasure rose to the surface. They were foreordained to be at that place where they met the person they would marry. They were predestined to go through the pain that eventually led to the hunger that caused them to go looking for the kingdom: to ask, seek and knock until the door opened. They were chosen from the beginning of the world to hear that sermon or read that book or meet that person or think that thought, or whatever it was that caused the light to glint off the gold, the diamond, the pearl that let them know that *they* were God's treasure. Treasured so much that the Son of God would give everything — his very life for them.

Do you understand this? Do you understand that this kingdom is something you must look for? Ask for? Knock on every door for? Turn up every stone in the field for? Open every oyster for? And when you find it, it will cost you everything? And do you understand that you really don't find this kingdom so much as it finds you? Do you understand that you really can't give anything to enter this kingdom, because your way has been paid with the blood of Christ?

Do you understand what I am saying about the field and the merchant?

Do you understand that it doesn't matter if you understand, because the kingdom is like a net that picks up all of us regardless of whether we understand or not? And do you understand that it matters a great deal, that it is a matter of eternal life and eternal death to hear what Jesus is saying and hear his question, "Do you understand what I am saying?" and be able to answer "yes"?

---

1. Cox, Sidney, *A Swinger of Birches: A Portrait of Robert Frost*, (New York: New York University Press, 1957) p. 58.
2. Pearson, Carol S., *Awakening the Hero Within*, audiotape, (New York: Harper Audio, HarperCollins Publishers, 1991).

Prayer And Compassion Fatigue

They were tired and they needed a day off. The crowds kept getting larger. More and more sick people were being brought to Jesus and his disciples were getting burned out dealing with all that human misery. So Jesus declared a holiday. "Let's go camping," he said. At least that is what I think he said. Matthew makes it sound like he said, "Let's go off alone to a deserted place."

My guess is he got no arguments from his disciples. They took off their beepers, unplugged the phones and put up the "Closed for the Day" sign in the window. They got out the coolers, the tents, the sleeping bags and, of course, their fishing poles, put them into the boat and headed toward the undeveloped shore of Lake Galilee.

We can just imagine the conversation on that boat:

"Man, I'm goin' to spend the whole day just doin' nothin'."

"Whooee! The biggest problem I want to deal with today is whether I'm going to take a one hour nap or a two hour nap."

"I'll be so glad to get away from people and their problems. I don't want to talk to anyone today except the fish."

Of course, there's always one worrywart who feels guilty about taking a day off who says, "Yes, but people have so many needs and Jesus does them so much good."

19

The others have more sense: "Hey man, there's only so much to go around. Can't you see that Jesus is exhausted? *He's* the one who suggested this. After all, he's only human. We're all only human. We've got to take care of ourselves or we aren't going to do anybody else any good."

So they get to the other shore. Pull the boat up on the beach. Set up the tents. Somebody builds a fire. Somebody else starts tossing a frisbee around. The fishing poles are out and they are just tying their flies on to the end of their lines when the first people start showing up.

The disciples try to ignore them. Maybe they are just the people at the next campsite, but soon there are more and more and they come crowding down on to the beach and they are carrying people on stretchers, and some of them are hobbling on crutches and the disciples have the feeling that they aren't the campers on the other site.

You know how they felt when the crowd showed up ...

The two of you haven't had a night out without the kids in weeks. You finally get away. The waiter has just brought your appetizer when the baby-sitter calls and tells you the youngest has a high fever and has started throwing up.

You've been planning this vacation for six months. Your reservations are all made and three days before you are scheduled to go your mother calls and says your Dad is going to have a quadruple bypass as soon as the doctors can get his sugar stabilized.

You haven't had a day off in three weeks. Friday morning your sister calls, says her father-in-law has died and wonders if you could take her kids for the weekend.

It has been a very long day. You woke up before dawn because your arthritis hurt so much. You had to go to the grocery store and take your dog to the vet and on the way home your car started to act up and you had to leave it at the garage and get a taxi to take you home. All you want to do is go to bed when the phone rings and it's your friend who lost her husband last month and she just needs somebody to talk to.

And always, when we think we have given all we have to give there is always more need: the starving people in the midst of a famine; refugees from war; the devastation of floods, hurricanes, earth-quakes, and tornadoes; to say nothing of our neighbors who are hungry; the children who need someone to care about them; the youth in our community who have nowhere to go and nowhere to grow.

We know how the disciples felt. Matthew doesn't have to tell us. We know that they either felt frustrated and angry or they felt secretly pleased that they were so needed — or both.

Matthew doesn't have to tell us how the disciples felt. He does have to tell us how Jesus felt. He felt "compassion" for the crowd. That is, he felt what they felt. He felt the pain and desperation that would drive people to come so far to such an inconvenient place in the hope that they might find healing for their bodies and spirits and maybe even some meaning for their lives.

Matthew doesn't tell us what the disciples did. We know what they did. Some of them put on their false smiles and when people in the crowd apologized for interrupting their day off, they said, "Oh that's all right. Really! We weren't doing anything."

Others were less pleasant about it. "Come on! Now that you're here, get into line."

Others, the ones that were terrified at the prospect of having a whole day off with nothing to do, threw themselves into their crowd control mode and went about being aggressively helpful with all the sick people, proving once again that they were good and feeling once again that they were superior.

Matthew doesn't have to tell us what the disciples did.

Matthew does have to tell us what Jesus did.

Matthew says that Jesus cured people. He wasn't nice to them. He didn't harangue them and make them feel guilty because they had problems. He didn't take care of them in order to make himself feel superior and make them more dependent. He cured them. He gave the lame what they needed to stand on their own two feet. He gave the blind what they needed to see clearly again. He gave the deaf what they needed to be at peace with themselves. He gave the dying what they needed in order to live.

Then Matthew says when it was evening the disciples came to Jesus and finally said what they probably had wanted to say since the first person showed up that morning: "Send the crowds away."

In some ways that is one of our more honest prayers. We see the hungry on television or the homeless in our streets and something inside of us says, "Send these crowds of needy people away." Wouldn't the world be a better place without all this human need? A friend of mine loves to go to Disney World because "there aren't any poor people there." She thinks the world would be so wonderful and happy if it were just like Disney World.

"Send the crowds away" doesn't mean the crowds that go to Disney World or the crowds that show up at the mall on Sunday afternoon. We just want to send away the crowds of human need, and human need doesn't always come as a crowd. Sometimes we pray a modified form of this prayer about just one person, when a sick child wakes us up for the third time in the middle of the night, when we have been to the nursing home and heard the same old complaints for the hundredth time, when the phone rings and the voice on the other end is crying about her unhappy marriage, we pray our own modified prayer about sending the crowds away. Send John away; send Mother away; send Susie away. Just send them away to the villages round about so that they may find food — in other words, let them solve their own problems.

There's a lot to be said for that. We hear a lot about "co-dependency" these days and I alluded to it a few minutes ago when I mentioned those people who immerse themselves in other people's problems partly as a means of avoiding the pain of their own lives. Often the "good feeling" that we get when we help other people comes from the superiority we feel when we encounter people who seem to have problems that we don't have. "You are poor and I am not. You are sick and I am not. Your life is messed up and mine is not."

Wanting people to solve their own problems is a lot healthier than wanting to be a caretaker just because it makes us feel superior when people are dependent on us or it gives our lives meaning if we think we are indispensable.

So, in some ways, the prayer "send the crowds away so that they may go into the villages and buy food for themselves" is a healthy prayer. "Jesus, teach these people to take care of themselves."

Jesus, of course, answers their prayer. Jesus, of course, answers their prayer differently than they anticipated. Jesus always seems to answer our prayers differently than we anticipate. He says, "You give them something to eat."

Now how is that an answer to the prayer, "Send the crowds away so that they may buy food in the villages round about?"

It is an answer because, as we have already seen, the real prayer, the underlying prayer — which is always the prayer God hears — is, "Eliminate human need by teaching people to take care of themselves."

How is Jesus' answer, "you give them something to eat," an answer to the prayer, "Eliminate human need by teaching people to take care of themselves?"

Listen to the story. The disciples complain that they can't give this crowd something to eat. There must be over 5,000 men here plus their wives and kids. We are talking a baseball stadium full of people. That's a lot of hot dogs.

Jesus says, "What's in the cooler?"

The disciples say, "Five loaves of bread and two fish."

He tells them, "Bring them here to me," and when the disciples bring them, Jesus does exactly what he would do at the Last Supper. He looked up to heaven, blessed the food, broke it up into small pieces and gave it to the disciples. The disciples then distributed it to the crowd.

There is a lot of speculation about what really happened next. Some say the bread and the fish just kept miraculously multiplying. The daughter of a missionary once told me about a barrel of flour that the mission board sent every three months to her family as part of their support. Transportation was so uncertain and the mission board's finances were so shaky that sometimes it took four months or more for the next flour barrel to come. Every day her mother would go to the barrel and scoop out flour but never look in to see how much was left. She never ran out of flour, no matter how long it took for the next flour barrel to arrive.

The world is full of stories like that, so I don't doubt that Jesus could have miraculously multiplied the loaves and the fish. I am also intrigued by another theory, however. That is the one that suggests that people in the crowd had brought food with them, but nobody wanted to bring it out and eat it because they figured nobody else had any and they would have to share and there wouldn't be enough for them and their family. When the disciples shared what they had, people were inspired to share their food, too and it turned out to be like one of our church pot-luck dinners. Everybody brings a dish large enough to feed their own family, puts it on the table and somehow we have so much food that we all eat too much and there is plenty left over.

Either way, it is a miracle. A rather ordinary miracle in a way. An everyday miracle. It's a miracle that as many people get fed in this world as do every day. The greater miracle is the miracle of empowerment.

Jesus empowered his disciples to work a miracle, this every-day miracle of feeding people. They didn't know it then, but he was answering their prayer, "Eliminate this human need by having people take care of themselves." He was answering their prayer by teaching his disciples that they could not only take care of themselves but that they had the power to do far more for others than they ever dreamed.

The only people who can really help other people are the ones who have themselves overcome helplessness. Only the empowered can empower others and empowerment is the only real help there is. Yes, some people have some real physical and mental limitations and they need our aid. Yes, some people are hungry today and they need to be fed.

Small children need to be cared for, but small children need to be taught, day-by-day, that they have the power to take care of themselves. They need to be taught to hold a spoon and a fork and to feed themselves and the only one who can do that is someone who has learned how to use a spoon and a fork. They need to be taught to tie their own shoes and the only one who can do that is someone who has learned to tie his or her shoes. They need to gradually make more and more of their own decisions, handle more and more of their own emotional issues and the only one who can do that is someone who has taken charge of his or her own life. Children need to be empowered.

The sick need to be empowered. Dr. Bernie Siegel says so many true things about taking charge of one's own life, even when we are ill. Yes, he says, that does involve asking people to help you with your shopping, or driving you to the doctor if you need it. It also means questioning what the doctor is prescribing; thinking through what kind of treatment is right for you; being in charge of your illness instead of letting your illness be in charge of you.

Some friends of mine have a son who has severe dyslexia. They spent thousands of dollars that they could ill afford on a minister's salary to send him to a special school that taught him that he wasn't a problem. He was a person with a problem and he could be in charge of that problem.

Sometimes our prayer, "Send the crowds away," is even about ourselves. "Send my problem away. Eliminate my needs." And the answer comes back, "You give them something to eat. *You* do something about it. *You* handle it."

When we say, "We can't," Jesus asks us what we have, what our resources are.

Sometimes our greatest resource is the knowledge that we have overcome problems in the past. Sometimes the best thing we have to give others is that knowledge. We did it and so can you. We fed 5,000 people with five loaves and two fish. So can you.

Gloria Steinem tells about the Confidence Clinic, a group of single mothers and other women who were divorced, widowed, deserted and often on welfare who opened a clinic for women in similar circumstances in rural southwestern Oregon. They couldn't get government funding because they weren't "professionals." They were just women who had been through it and they offered a 12-week program in job skills, legal rights, survival as a single parent, money management and even a clothes bank so that women could dress up appropriately for job interviews. Ninety-eight percent of the women who went through the program who had dropped out of high school earned their diplomas in those 12 weeks. Within a year, most were employed or in training for a specific job or in college.[1]

Jesus solved the problem of human need by empowering the disciples to meet their own need — their need to eliminate the need of the crowd — and, having been so empowered, they taught others the same thing. They actually began to see the world differently, which is the key to empowerment.

There is that famous opening scene in the movie *The Wizard of Oz*. We see Dorothy's life in Kansas all in black-and-white, which was what audiences in 1939 were used to. Then, when the tornado blows her and Toto and her house "somewhere over the rainbow," Dorothy opens the door on Oz and suddenly everything is in color.

That's what Jesus does for us when we take stock of our resources in the face of any need and put them into his hands and then go ahead in faith with what we have. Our eyes are opened to just how powerful he is — how abundant the resources of God are. I know that this sounds like pie-in-the-sky to the person who feels burned out this morning. But I urge you, as you come to this table to receive this bread, to think what it would be to take what little you have and give it to solving some personal or family or global problem that seems overwhelming to you. Do it and see what happens. Amen.

---

1. Steinem, Gloria, *Revolution From Within*, (Boston: Little, Brown and Co., 1992) pp. 177-178.

Why Not Walk On What Jesus Walked On When He Walked On Water?

I wish Matthew, Mark and John had consulted me before they wrote their gospels. If they had only sent me their rough drafts, I could have put a big red "X" through this story about Jesus walking on the water. (Luke apparently had a good editor. He didn't include this story.) I would have written a note in the margin stating that I think it would be best not to include this story because it would cause two kinds of reactions in the twentieth century: some people would laugh at it, and others would take it so seriously that they would waste all their time trying to reconcile it with science and completely miss the point of the story.

The jokesters have had a field day with this story. Someone confronted with a body of water barring his way and no bridge or boat to get across may joke about putting on his "J.C. shoes" in order to amble over the aquatic depths. Proud grandparents are sometimes accused of bragging that their grandchild's first steps were across the surface of the family bathtub.

I guess I prefer some of that light-heartedness to the heavy-handedness of those who take the details of the story so seriously that they feel they have to explain it and wind up explaining it away.

For example, some interpreters in the first half of this century suggested that Jesus followed a sand bar that stretched out into the lake which just happened to end right next to the disciples' boat. One wonders why these experienced fishermen didn't notice it, or think of it when they saw Jesus walking toward them. Why did they think he was a ghost? Why didn't they say, "I'll bet Jesus is walking on a sand bar in almost total darkness!"

Others say that the laws of nature were suspended or that laws were operating that we don't understand. As Saint Augustine said in the fourth century A.D., "Miracles are not a contradiction of nature. They are only in contradiction to what we know of nature."

There is something to be said for that attitude. Sometimes, Bible scholars who can read several dead languages but cannot program their VCRs are pretty cavalier about saying something is "scientifically impossible" when more and more physicists and chemists and biologists are reasoning that if the universe is infinite and is full of an infinite number of possibilities, who are we to say that anything is impossible? About all we can say is that some things are more probable than others. Maybe, under circumstances that we haven't been able to replicate experimentally, it is possible to increase the surface tension of water (which is what we are talking about when we talk about "breaking the surface" of water). Maybe it would be possible to increase that surface tension to the point that it would bear the weight of a full-grown man. It isn't highly probable, but who is to say that it is impossible?

However, spending all day trying to explain this miracle scientifically misses the point. When we ask, "What did Jesus walk on when he walked on water?" we aren't asking a scientific question. We are asking a religious question. It is a question that has to do with faith, at least that is the way Jesus framed it when he hauled a dripping-wet Peter out of the water and asked him what happened to his faith.

For a moment there, Peter did walk on water like Jesus did. Then he began to sink and Jesus said it was because he lacked faith.

This strange nighttime incident did not take place to make us speculate about the natural forces that bind water molecules together. It took place to make the disciples — and us — ask, what is faith? The answer, the obvious answer, is that faith is what you walk on when whatever else you are walking on isn't enough to hold you up.

Jesus concludes the Sermon on the Mount by saying: "Everyone then who hears these words of mine and acts on them will be like a wise man who built his house on rock. The rain fell, the floods came, and the winds blew and beat on that house, but it did not fall, because it had been founded on rock. And everyone who hears these words of mine and does not act on them will be like a foolish man who built his house on sand. The rain fell, and the floods came, and the winds blew and beat against that house, and it fell — and great was its fall!" (Matthew 7:24-27).

Water and sand have this in common: You can sink in both of them.

Peter, whose name was the Greek word for *rock*, sank just like a rock when he tried to walk on water. But for a moment, Peter walked on something . . . something that was as solid as a rock, and Jesus said that something was faith.

Faith is the foundation of life. If you don't want to sink, walk on faith. If you don't want your life to fall apart, like a house built on sand, build your life on faith.

Faith in what?

Faith in the word of God.

And what is the word of God?

There are really three answers to that. The word of God is the Bible. The Word of God is Jesus Christ, who is the Word made flesh. The word of God is also the still, small voice that speaks in our hearts. It is the Holy Spirit in our hearts, crying, "Abba! Father." They are all connected. The Bible, we Christians believe, points to Jesus Christ, who is that invisible, spiritual word of God in visible, physical, historical form.

All that I have just said is nothing but theological theory, however, until we voluntarily give up our faith in everything else and step out in faith on the word of God, just as Peter stepped out of the boat that night. When Peter stepped out of that boat, he did or was attempting to do what Jesus had already done when He was alone on the mountain.

Let us return to the beginning of this strange story about Jesus walking on the water. Jesus has just fed over 5,000 people with five loaves and two fish — actually his disciples have fed the crowd by placing their five loaves and two fish in the hands of Jesus. Immediately after the crowd has been fed — immediately, Matthew emphasizes that it was *immediately* afterward — Jesus, first of all, sends the disciples off in their boat and then he sends the crowd away. Now this is a very odd thing. We might compare it to the seventh game of the World Series in which the team playing in its home stadium is down three runs in the bottom half of the ninth inning. The bases are loaded but there are also two outs. The next batter hits a home run and then immediately after crossing home plate sends all of his teammates into the locker room and tells the whole crowd to please leave quietly. Why would anyone do that? Why would anyone not enjoy the adulation, the cheers, the victory celebration that would naturally follow? Why would anyone run away from the champagne that would be poured over his head? The microphones that would be shoved in his face? The babies and the candy bars that would be named after him that day? No one in his right mind would send all those people away unless, of course, he was trying to save his soul. For "what will [you] gain by winning the whole world at the cost of [your] true self? Or what can [you] give that will buy that self back?" (Matthew 16:26 NEB).

Do you remember how, right after he was baptized, Jesus went out and fasted in the wilderness, perhaps the very one he was in right now, and after 40 days the devil came and tempted him to turn stones into bread, to perform a spectacular miracle, and to become the ruler of the world? Well, Jesus had just created bread. He had performed a spectacular miracle and John's gospel tells us that the crowd wanted to make him king (John 6:15).

Jesus went up to the mountain to hang on to his soul. To let go of the temptations to bask in the adulation and the power that the miracle he just performed could give him.

Most of us can't even begin to understand that. We have been taught that success and adulation and power are such desirable things that we could never imagine giving them up voluntarily.

Neither, I think, could the disciples imagine it. That is why Jesus sent them off in the boat even before he sent off the crowd. After all, the disciples had been integral performers in the miracle. They were the ones who came up with the five loaves and two fish. They were the ones who distributed the bread. They were the ones who picked up the leftovers.

My guess is that they were pretty high on themselves when they started rowing across the lake. We can imagine them saying to each other, "Whooee, did you see that?"

"Yeah man, but I can still hardly believe it."

"Can you imagine what we could do with that kind of power?"

"Yeah, we could feed the world!"

"People would come to us from all over!"

"Our pictures will be in all the papers!"

"We'll be interviewed on *60 Minutes*."

"Won't the Romans try to stop us?"

"Hey! Let them just try. What do the Romans have to offer that's better than a free meal everyday? Even their soldiers will want that."

"Yeah! And if they wanted to eat, they would have to do what *we* say."

"Wouldn't it be wrong for us to use military power like that?"

"Not if we are on God's side, and we obviously are or we couldn't have performed that miracle."

"We'll be more powerful than Caesar!"

"We'll be the kings of the world!"

They would be so busy imagining how powerful they would be and congratulating themselves on their close relationship with God that the future kings of the world wouldn't notice that the wind had picked up and that they weren't going anywhere. After a while someone might say, "Man, it seems like we've been rowing for hours, when are we going to get there?" Somebody else might say, "We *have* been rowing for hours. My back is killing me. What's going on?"

Somebody might finally figure it out. "We aren't getting anywhere because the wind is too strong."

The others, especially the experienced fishermen, might scoff at that. "What do you mean, it's too strong? I've been fishing on this lake all my life. Sure, sometimes you really have to put your back into it, but I've never seen a wind I can't handle. Come on, you sissies, start rowing and quit yakking."

So they row harder and harder and the wind picks up stronger and stronger. The waves are starting to slam into the boat, rolling it and getting them wet. Matthew doesn't paint a life-threatening situation. This doesn't appear to be the same kind of storm as the one that so terrified the disciples that they woke up Jesus so that he could still it. Matthew just says, "They were fighting the wind."

Now there's a descriptive phrase. There are times in most of our lives when we don't seem to be getting anywhere. There are things in life that we can't seem to make any headway against. Sometimes it takes us a while to wake up to that fact. We think we are sailing along quite nicely. We may even be pretty pleased with ourselves. We may have a string of home runs to our credit. We may even have just pulled off a miracle or two. We've gotten the promotions. We have the nice home, the well-behaved kids, the car and the van parked in the driveway. Our health has always been good.

Then the weather changes almost imperceptibly at first and then we begin to notice that something is different. Some notice it at work. Whatever we chart on the graph of success — increases in prestige or pay checks, numbers of compliments or customers, profits or professional recognition — whatever we chart starts to flatten out.

Some notice it at home. The number of arguments seems to increase. The emotional temperature is a few degrees lower.

Some notice it within themselves. It takes a couple more cups of coffee to get going in the morning and maybe a couple more drinks to wind down at night. We put on weight. We don't laugh as much. We pray and nothing seems to get through the ceiling. That doggone lump under the arm isn't going away. The face in the mirror looks older every day.

Hey! we think; this is no big deal. A temporary thing. Have I ever met a challenge I couldn't handle? I'll just put in a few more hours at work. I'll take a seminar. I'll try a new time management system.

I'll try to be more thoughtful of my spouse. I'll spend more time with the kids.

I'll go on a diet. I'll do some positive thinking. I'll get up an hour earlier in order to pray. I'll get my hair dyed or transplanted. I'll make a rule about how much I drink or smoke or eat and I'll just keep to it. That's all it takes, a little discipline. I'll ask the doctor about that lump the next time I see her. I can handle it. There's nothing to worry about.

And sometimes, that's right. That's all it takes. Sometimes it isn't. Sometimes we find ourselves rowing and rowing against the wind. The harder we try, the more some kind of resistance seems to build up on the other side and we are stuck.

That's a humbling experience. All that power we thought we had, all that control we thought we had was just an illusion. Sure, we may have done some great things, some wonderful things, some miraculous things, but the more we row against the wind the clearer it becomes to us that we were the recipients of grace and not the exercisers of great power, because rowing against the wind doesn't make us feel powerful. It makes us feel powerless. Maybe we did hit that home run in the bottom half of the ninth inning, but that was yesterday. Today, this morning, it isn't even dawn yet, it's still dark and we row and we row and we aren't getting anywhere. Our own strength is not sufficient.

That thought no sooner comes to us than a shadowy figure appears. "No," we think. "I don't believe it. It can't be. I'll ignore it. I'll ignore the vision. I'll ignore the thought." We don't have to be on the Sea of Galilee to notice that shadowy figure. It's just as we start to give up on ourselves that the eyes of our souls are able to discern that there might be something out there that we can't explain, that we can't control, that we can't even really identify yet.

The thought that there might *really* be a spiritual dimension to the universe is at first a terrifying thought. I mean when it *really* occurs to us that there is a spiritual dimension. I'm not talking about piety here. I'm not talking about religion. Too often religion is one of the shields we use to ward off the fact that the spiritual realm is real. We are terrified of the spiritual realm. It seems as dark and murky and unpredictable as midnight on the Sea of Galilee. It seems ghostly. Yet, out of the spiritual realm comes a voice that says "Take heart, it is I; do not be afraid."

A perceptive Bible scholar says that one point of this story is to teach us that Jesus is not like us. Oh, he is, he is. He was flesh and blood, just like us. He knew all of our temptations. He felt all of our pain. At the same time, he is not like us. He can walk on water. He can do what we cannot do. Therefore, he is able to help us when we cannot help ourselves. Jesus comes to us out of the spiritual realm and he is able to help us when no human being in the world can help us. But how do we get to him? How do we reach his helping hand? Peter says, "Lord, if it is you, command me to come to you on the water."

And Jesus says, "Come."

Where is Jesus? Jesus is in the spiritual realm and where is the spiritual realm? It is in the future. That is why it seems so dark and murky and ghostly. We cannot see very far or very clearly into the future. We do know that the future holds our own death and the deaths of those we love. The future is scary, yet the voice of Jesus calls to us and says, "Be not afraid." He assures us that in that darkness and in that murkiness, he is there and he calls us to come to him.

There is that most intriguing passage from the first letter of John: "Beloved, we are God's children now; what we will be has not yet been revealed. What we do know is this: when he is revealed, we will be like him, for we will see him as he is" (1 John 3:2).

Can you imagine being like Jesus? Can you imagine having faith enough to move mountains or to walk on water or to heal the sick or to make any sacrifice? He comes to us precisely when we are rowing against the wind and making no headway toward the goals we have chosen. He calls to us out of the future. He tells us not to be afraid and he gives us a new goal — himself. He calls us to come to him.

Some get out of the boat and test the water. Some take a step or two into that future. As millions of sermons have said, Peter was okay as long as he had his eyes on Jesus. It was when he looked at the waves that he began to sink. Then Jesus pulled him out and asked, "You of little faith, why did you doubt?"

There is a note of sadness in that question. We have the sense that not just Peter, but maybe humanity itself missed an opportunity to move to a new level of faith. I said earlier that one point of this story is to show that Jesus is not like us, but Peter's excursion on the water, as short as it is, implies that we can become like Jesus — except we don't. We are people of little faith. What hope is there for us? Our only hope is Jesus.

A missionary once had to cross a river on a plank of wood to reach the place where he was to preach. He hesitated. His hosts urged him, saying that hundreds of people had crossed the plank that day ahead of him. The missionary argued that, as a westerner, he was probably bigger and heavier than anyone else. His hosts, to reassure him, sent two strong men together out on the plank, which bore their weight easily. So the missionary slowly and hesitantly crossed the river on the plank. When he reached the other side, his hosts asked him why he hadn't just taken their word and trusted their judgment.

The missionary replied, "Because my faith is weak. It wasn't the strength of my faith that took me across, but the strength of the plank."

It isn't the strength of our faith that we walk on in life. It's the strength of Jesus' faith. Amen.

Proper 15
Pentecost 13
Ordinary Time 20
Matthew 15: (10-20) 21-28 (C)
Matthew 15: 21-28 (L, RC)

Love Without Limits

The epitaph on the grave of Albert Camus, who won the Nobel Prize for Literature in 1957, reads: "Here I understand what they call glory: the right to love without limits."

In our gospel lesson we see two people who love without limits. Neither of them seem very glorious. One is a tired itinerant preacher named Jesus. The other is a woman who has no name — only a racial designation: a Canaanite woman. "Canaanite" was to the Jews of Jesus' time what "Native American" is to the majority of North Americans. The Canaanites were the people from whom the ancestors of the Jews took their land. The dialogue that takes place between them doesn't seem very loving, at least not at first. In fact, it may be the most unloving portrait of Jesus in the gospels.

As their dialogue proceeds we see each of them breaking through the limits of love.

The woman begins by shouting, "Have mercy on me, Lord, Son of David; my daughter is tormented by a demon." We don't exactly know what that means. We do know that it is not something that people usually went around shouting about. I don't know if you have ever had a child who had a problem. I'm not talking about a broken arm or the chicken pox. I'm talking about a mental

37

problem or a behavioral problem or an addiction. If you have, you know something about the limits this woman's love had to break through to shout this at Jesus. You know how, first of all, you have to love your child enough to admit to yourself that something isn't right. You have to quit saying to yourself, "This is something he'll grow out of. This is just a stage she's going through." If you think that is easy, you haven't done it, because it may mean that there is something wrong with *you*: your genes, your parenting, your own emotional well-being.

The next limitation this mother's love had to break through was her belief that she could handle whatever was wrong herself. Sometimes it's true. A parent's love and a parent's wisdom can work a lot of miracles. All we need to do is pay attention, figure out what's wrong and find ways to help our child. That's the way most parents do most of their parenting. We get used to the idea that nothing is going to come along that we cannot handle. But sometimes things do come along that we can't handle. Parents try to do all they can to make an anorexic daughter eat, but nothing works. Parents try to make rules to structure the life of an alcoholic teenager:

"You are to be in by this hour."

"No liquor in the house."

"You have to account for every last penny we give you."

The alcoholic finds ways to drink that are beyond our control. It's tough to admit that we can't do for our children what they need.

It's tough to ask for help for ourselves. It may be even tougher to admit that we need help with our children.

On top of that, there are some things that it's all right for our kids to have wrong with them and there are other things that are not all right. People talk loudly about how many times they've sent their child's orthodontist to Europe or how often their children lose their contacts. They don't talk loudly about how many AA meetings their son goes to each week, or how often their daughter's stomach has had to be pumped.

It takes a lot of love to ask for help, especially if it means that the neighbors will know about it. It means breaking down the limits pride puts on love. That's what this woman did. She swallowed her pride and started shouting out so that everyone could hear the secret she had been hiding from everyone: "Have mercy on me, Lord, Son of David; my daughter is tormented by a demon."

This woman comes to Jesus with a problem. Her daughter needs healing. This is not unusual. The gospel gives the impression that people came to Jesus all day long with similar problems, but Matthew says, "[Jesus] did not answer her at all."

If you have ever finally gotten up the courage to ask someone for help, you can imagine how devastating this must have been to this woman.

There is hardly any bitterness worse than the bitterness of people who asked for help from their church or their pastor and were ignored. Dr. John Savage did a study of why people who were once active in the church — I mean, the kind of people who sing in the choir, teach Sunday school and serve on committees as well as attend worship almost every Sunday — why people like that drop out, quit coming and eventually ask to be taken off the rolls. He found that there were a variety of reasons, but often people had a story about some time when they asked for help, or they felt that their need for help was so apparent that they didn't need to ask for it, and they were ignored. He said that as he interviewed these people, most of them found it very difficult to tell this story and, when they did, they would almost always cry — men as well as women — even though the incident may have happened over a decade earlier. It hurts that much to cry for help and be ignored.

Being human and a pastor, I know I probably have ignored cries for help. Let me drop the "probably." I know I have. I'm not even counting the ones where I was expected to read people's minds or somehow know that people were in the hospital when they didn't even tell their best friends, to say nothing of calling the church office. I know I have ignored people for a number of reasons. Sometimes I have done it because I was tired. Sometimes I've done it because I was preoccupied with my own problems or other issues that seemed bigger and I lost my sense of perspective. Sometimes I've ignored people because I told myself that I probably couldn't help anyway. Sometimes I've ignored people because I told myself that they weren't my responsibility. They weren't officially members of my church. They were asking for something that didn't fit my definition of what a minister does.

I'm not telling you this to tell you that I'm a bad person. I really try to be a conscientious and caring pastor. Honesty compels me to say that I am only human and being only human I'm going to miss things. I'm going to make decisions about what I'm going to do and what I'm not going to do because there are only so many hours in a day and there is only so much of me to go around. I'm going to make some of those decisions consciously and some of them unconsciously. All human beings do. The administrator of a large mental-health clinic which employed many counselors once described what he called the BYMF factor. A BYMF is a Beautiful Young Male or Female. He noted that whenever an attractive-looking young adult entered the clinic, the receptionist immediately gave that person attention and was more detailed in giving directions. The intake person also tended to see the attractive young adult more promptly and appeared to give more thought about an appropriate match-up with a counselor. Elderly people, people who were not attractive, people who were obviously poor, or who were of a minority race got considerably less attention, were more likely to wait longer at the receptionist's desk, had a more perfunctory intake interview and often had to wait longer to get an appointment with a counselor. All of this happened in a place where people were committed to accepting everyone impartially and unconditionally. They would swear up and down that everyone got equal treatment regardless of race, creed, color, class, gender or age. However, if you have ever been or are now of the wrong race, color, class, gender or age, you know that you get treated differently and you are ignored more than people who are younger, whiter, have straighter teeth, are wealthier or are male.

It's human nature to prefer some people to others. The question we have to ask as we read this passage is, "Was Jesus only human?" Did he share our prejudices about people? Did he consciously or unconsciously prefer some people to others? That's a tough question, but it is a question that we have to face squarely whenever we read this passage. Some suggest that Jesus was deliberately testing the woman's faith. Other commentators ask us to hear the humor in the voices of both Jesus and the woman when he says to her, "It is not fair to take the children's food and throw it to the dogs," and she replies: "Yes, Lord, yet even the dogs eat the crumbs that fall from their masters' table." Jesus was only joking, they say, and the woman "got it" and joined in the repartee.

Either theory is possible. We certainly don't want a prejudiced Jesus, do we? Or do we? Don't prejudiced people need a savior, too? The fact is, everybody is prejudiced. The biggest liars in the world are the people who say that they aren't racist or sexist or prejudiced against people of different social classes or of different ages. The reason I say that so categorically is because the people I know who work hardest at overcoming those barriers — people who are really working on creating better relations between the races or making systems fairer to persons of both sexes — are the people who seem to be most aware of their own racism or sexism. The dean of a predominantly white seminary which was building a model program in black studies, a white man married to a black woman, once said that every time he thinks he has rid himself of racism, he finds another canister hidden inside his heart.

People who say that they love all people just the same are so superficial that they aren't worth talking to. They haven't begun to learn about love. My guess is that they haven't even confronted the difficulty of loving someone of a different sex; a wife or a husband; or a person of a different age; a child or a parent; to say nothing of what it means to love someone of a different color or culture.

To be human is to be prejudiced. Some people may have better reason to be prejudiced than others. In order to understand Jesus' remark about food for the children going to the dogs, we have to understand how fiercely he felt about his mission to the Jewish people. The Jews were a minority group. They had been kicked around for centuries by other nations who were bigger and richer. In some ways, Jesus was like Malcolm X, who decided that the only way black people were going to achieve any dignity was to do everything for themselves. There is a scene in the motion picture, *The Autobiography of Malcolm X*, in which Malcolm X is walking across a college campus on the way to a lecture. A young white woman sees him and runs after him trying to get his attention. Malcolm X strides on, trying to ignore her, but she runs out in front of him and backpedals as she tries to ask him what she, a white person who sincerely cares about good racial relations, can do to help black people. Malcolm X stops for a moment, looks directly at her and coldly says, "Nothing!" Then he marches on.

That's a little bit like the way Jesus felt about his mission to the Jews. His mission was to his own people. Other people were a distraction.

But Jesus . . . Jesus was perfect, wasn't he? At the very least — or the very most — he was perfect in love. After all, he was the Son of God and God loves everybody. Yes, he was the Son of God and he was also the Son of Man. In fact he was much more likely to call himself the Son of Man than the Son of God. Centuries ago, we Christians decided that we have to live with a logical contradiction when we talk about Jesus. He was completely God and he was completely human.

In order to affirm that, I have to believe that Jesus of Nazareth had to push through the limitations of his own prejudices in order to really love other people just as much as you and I have to push through our prejudices in order to love other people. I also affirm that God was active in whatever Jesus said and did.

When I read about Jesus ignoring this woman and speaking coldly to her, telling her that it is not right to give the children's food to dogs, I affirm that God was in Christ somehow testing this woman's faith as all of us have our faith tested now and then when we ask for help from God and/or from God's people and either we feel ignored or the answer seems to be "no."

The temptation then is to give up on God, give up on the church, give up on other people, or give up on ourselves. It is then that only love, in this case the woman's love for her daughter, can break through the limitation of fear and despair — call it the limitation of believing that some things are impossible.

Everybody needs that kind of love. I once overheard a conversation between a mother and her six-year-old son. The six-year-old had recently been blessed with a new baby brother. One day, as his mother was working in the kitchen, she picked up his little brother and held him close to her. I guess, even at his advanced age the six-year-old was a little jealous, so he asked his mother a hypothetical question: "Mommy, could you pick me up?"

At first she dismissed it by saying, "You're too big to pick up," but then she said something that surprised me, "but I could pick you up if your life depended on it." Well, now this was a new thought! So he decided to push it to its logical conclusion: "Could you pick up Daddy if his life depended on it?" Now his father was 6'2" and his mother was only 5'4" but she said, "Yes, if his life depended on it, I could and I would pick him up." The little boy seemed to be deeply reassured. He was loved with a love that would do the impossible if called upon.

The Canaanite woman decided to believe in a love that would do the impossible to save her daughter. She decided to believe in a love that would cross all barriers. Part of the reason she believed is that she loved her daughter with that kind of love. She knew it was impossible to get help from this Jewish man who had been taught from birth to ignore someone like her. Yet she refused to accept that anything was impossible when it came to her daughter's welfare.

Now I know I'm on dangerous ground, but I frankly believe that the human being in Jesus grew in his confrontation with that woman. After all, Luke tells us that Jesus grew in wisdom and stature and in favor with God and people. One of the discoveries of adulthood is that we always have to keep growing or we start dying. If Jesus was fully human, why should he be any different?

I mentioned *The Autobiography of Malcolm X* a few minutes ago. Toward the end of the movie, Malcolm X, who was a Muslim, made a pilgrimage to Mecca. On the pilgrimage he found people of all colors and races who believed as he believed and that experience caused him to grow. He came back a different man, more open to working with people of all races toward a common goal of justice. He was beginning to learn how to love without limits.

There is no glory greater than the glory of loving without limits. There are no obstacles that any of us will overcome in life that are more difficult or more important than the obstacles to love:

43

the obstacle of pride, the obstacle of prejudice, and the obstacle of despair. The most difficult things in the world are to swallow our pride, open up to people who are different than we are, and to believe that God's love is so great that it can and will do the impossible, even raise the dead, for our sake and for the sake of the people we love. The good news is, love is so great that it can overcome even those difficulties. Amen.

**Proper 16
Pentecost 14
Ordinary Time 21
Matthew 16:13-20**

The Rock Of Faith

Most libraries divide popular novels into categories: westerns, mysteries, romance, spy novels and science fiction. The novels in those categories follow a certain formula. I'm watching to see if a library will someday have a shelf for the threat-to-Christianity novel. The threat-to-Christianity novel is one in which the hero has discovered a document that proves that Christianity is false. Sometimes it's a fifth gospel or a letter from Jesus written in his old age or some incontrovertible evidence that the whole Bible was made up. The hero is pursued mercilessly by secret agents of the Vatican, terrorists hired by the Orthodox Patriarch of Constantinople, and thugs employed by televangelists, all of whom are aided and abetted by the governments of the world who recognize that, if this news leaks out, Christianity will be destroyed and the moral fabric of Western Civilization, which is already paper-thin, will be torn into shreds and chaos will reign.

I've always wondered why these books even get published, besides the obvious fact that they always have the necessary mixture of sex and violence. I can't see why anyone buys the basic premise of the plot — the idea that a "scientific discovery" could disprove the Christian faith. But people do believe it.

I suspect we believe it for two reasons. First of all, because the church looks like a house of cards built on a coffee table with one short leg, rather than a rock which even death cannot conquer. Second, because we have the mistaken belief that Christianity is based on some logical assumptions which, if they could be proved wrong, would cause the whole structure of the Christian faith to collapse. Actually, it is helpful for us to examine some of these false ideas about the foundations of Christianity.

Some things really do give the impression of shakiness. The empires of the televangelists have come and gone quickly. Does that prove that Christianity is a house of cards? No, it only proves that the rock on which Christ builds the church is not a charming television personality.

Many of the famous churches in our cities, which once boasted thousands of members and had ministers whose names were known all over the country, are now just handfuls of people meeting in huge sanctuaries that feel like mausoleums. Does that prove that Christianity is a house of cards? No, it only proves that the rock on which Christ built his church is not Marble Collegiate, nor Old Stone Presbyterian, nor Methodist stucco, nor Lutheran brick and Episcopal limestone.

Along with that decline has been the decline in the church's influence in our society. A survey of clergy morale showed that ministers who began their ministries in the 1950s and early '60s felt that ministers were more respected members of the community three or four decades ago than they are now. [1] Communities that used to set aside all day Sunday and Wednesday evenings for church activities now schedule youth sports programs on Sunday morning. Two generations ago, most people went to church or they knew the name of the church they were staying away from. Does that prove that Christianity is a house of cards? No, it only proves that Christ did not found the church on the rock of power and influence and public acceptance.

Those who have more than a superficial understanding of Christianity know that it is founded on something we call "faith." However, many of the people who believe that Christianity could be disproved are like the authors of these books — people who are on the outside looking in. What those outsiders see, too often, is a lot of people inside the church who, in fact, think that they have to defend God and the Christian faith against changes brought about by new understandings of history or of the natural world or of human nature. They see a Roman Catholic hierarchy which waited until 1993 to forgive Galileo for looking through his telescope and discovering that the earth moved around the sun instead of the other way around. They see Protestants trying to get schools to teach something called Creation Science which insists that the world is no more than 6,000 years old and if rocks and fossils say otherwise, the rocks and fossils are lying. These folks think the Christian faith is based on the infallible authority of the church and its leadership or on the infallible authority of a literal reading of the Bible.

This passage that we have just read from Matthew's gospel tells us that the church is founded on a rock. What is that rock? Let's look closely at this pivotal passage and see if we can discern what Jesus meant by the rock — the foundation on which the Christian church and all its beliefs are founded. In the passage, Jesus renames his disciple, Simon, calling him "Peter" which is an English version of the Greek word for rock. One of the intriguing things about this passage is that Matthew uses the masculine form of the Greek word for rock, *Petros*, for Peter's name — obviously because Peter is a man — but he uses the feminine form, *petra*, when he reports that Jesus said, "Upon this rock I will build my church." This rock on which the church will be built is feminine. The repetition of the word *rock* for Peter's name and for the foundation of the church indicates that Peter is, indeed, the foundation of the church; this flesh-and-blood person, this fisherman from Galilee who had a wife and a mother-in-law, and a house and a boat. Yet the variation in gender says that the rock is something that is not quite Peter.

For one thing, Peter will die someday. He was a man. He did die. We have a very strong and reliable tradition that he died a martyr, possibly crucified as Jesus was. However, the rock which is the foundation of the church is something that death cannot hold. The rock is Peter, but the rock is something about Peter that the gates of Hades will not prevail against. To put it more clearly, the rock is something the doors of Death will not be able to keep in. "Hades" is not hell, the realm of evil and Satanic forces, it is Death (with a capital "D").

Both Protestants and Catholics have understood that Jesus meant something that could not be completely identified with the man Peter. Catholics have said it is an institution that Jesus set up — a leadership position that we now call the Papacy. Protestants have said that it is something less tangible than that — the rock is Peter's faith, it is the revelation that Peter received from God which told him that Jesus is the Christ. That faith is the rock on which the church rests.

Is there an answer as to what the rock is? Well, first of all, let me state the obvious, the rock that Jesus is talking is . . . a rock. I started by talking about how people inside the church think that they have to protect God and the Christian faith and people outside the church have the impression that Christianity is a very vulnerable thing — a house of cards built on a shaky card table. Rocks are not vulnerable. Rocks are not shaky. Rocks are solid.

Where is the rock? Where is Peter? Peter is wherever there is a person who believes so much that Jesus is the Christ that his or her confidence in Christ encourages and supports the community that Christ founded. That's where the rock is. The rock may be sitting on the throne of Peter in the Vatican making pronouncements that get reported in the newspapers of the world. The rock may also be sitting in a rocking chair in the church nursery singing "Jesus Loves Me" so that only a small baby hears.

We've recognized such rocks for years, only we don't call them rocks; we call them "pillars" — the pillars of the church. They are the people who have been there through thick and thin. The ones who have been a source of strength and courage and inspiration to others. The ones who, in one way or another, keep the church going.

Now you may say, "I know some of those pillars and they are not all nice people. Some of them can be cantankerous. They play power games. They are hypocritical sometimes. Some of them even ran away when the going got rough and then came back and took over again."

It is true that people have mixed motives for being pillars of the church. Some are shoring up their sense of self-righteousness; some are involved because the church will let them do some things that the rest of the world thinks they are not competent to do. Some are in it because they like to belong. But remember, we are talking about Peter. We are talking about the guy who was always pushing himself forward trying to be first. We are talking about the grandstander who wanted to walk on water just like Jesus. We are talking about the big-mouth who said he would die for Jesus and three hours later denied even knowing him. In other words, we are talking about a flawed human being like you and me. That's why Peter is so beloved by us all. I don't know any person with an ounce of honesty who doesn't identify with Peter. The rock on which Jesus founded the church was not a piece of polished marble. It was a big, stubborn, pock-marked piece of rock covered with moss. It may even have been the kind of rock that geologists call "conglomerate," which means that it is made up of smaller rock particles cemented together with hardened clay or sand. That's not a pretty rock; not the kind of rock that jewelers cut and polish, nor even the kind of rock that is selected to build cathedrals. In fact, one of the characteristics of the rock is that it doesn't fit in very well, even if it is a foundation stone.

The faith of Peter is a very individual faith. Jesus asked his disciples, "Who do people say that I am?" and they echoed the popular answers. Then he asked, "Who do *you* say that I am?" Peter offered an answer that hasn't been mentioned. "You are the Messiah, the Son of the Living God."

Jesus told Peter that he couldn't have known this because someone told it to him. It must have been revealed to him by heaven itself. Peter's faith is a first-hand faith. It is something he knows in his heart, rather than something he has heard with his ears or read in a book.

The people who become like Peter are people who know that Jesus is their savior. They know it in ways that you don't learn in Sunday school. A new pastor once sat in the office of a prominent member of his church. The man behind the desk told the minister that, in all honesty, he wasn't religious. He had been brought up in the church. He wanted his kids to be brought up in the church. He believed in the moral values of Christianity. He believed the church was good for the community, but he didn't believe in the supernatural claims of the church. Those were for the old ladies and the children. He was more honest than most people. He admitted that his faith, such as it was, was only second-hand.

Most people don't meet Jesus in a blinding flash of light, like Paul did on the Damascus road. Most of us meet Jesus the way Peter did. Jesus comes into our lives usually through someone else, just as Peter's brother, Andrew, introduced him to Jesus (John 1:41). So also, we have been introduced to Jesus through a parent or grandparent, a Sunday school teacher, a friend, a spouse or relative or neighbor or co-worker. He becomes a part of our lives, although it may be only a vague and distant part of our lives.

He may even ask us from time to time who we say that he is. If you were brought up like I was, you know all the right answers, "You are the Christ, the Son of God."

He will say to us, "But who do *you* say that I am?" We will say, "You are the Christ, the Son of God." He will shake his head. "No," he will say, "that is what you have been taught to say, that is what you think you are supposed to say, but you are still saying what other people say. Who do *you* say that I am?"

We are puzzled by that. We think we are speaking our convictions. Our heads tell us that we are speaking the truth. After all, we are saying what millions of people have believed for almost 2,000 years. "You are the Christ, the Son of God." What we don't realize, perhaps, is that we have internalized other people's opinions and beliefs and attitudes to the point we think they are our own. There is a sense in which all of us are brainwashed. That sounds harsh, but brainwashing is just the day-in, day-out repetition of certain ideas until we accept them without question. Some things have been repeated over and over again by our family, education and culture so that we have been conditioned to see things in a certain way, to think certain thoughts and hold to certain beliefs. One of the ways in which we know that we have been brainwashed about something is if we react with anger and fear at hearing our belief attacked.

You can be almost certain that the person who is most fanatical about "defending" Christianity is the person who thinks he believes what he has only heard other people say that they believe. Someone who cannot yet say, "Jesus is the Christ, the Son of God," from the depths of his own heart and his own experience.

Sometimes that experience comes through having to cope with one of life's most painful wounds and finding that Jesus, only Jesus, can heal that wound. Sometimes it happens that life just loses meaning and purpose and Jesus enters and gives it new direction. Sometimes it happens that we grow despairing about the state of the world and in Jesus we find a way to be part of the salvation of the world. Sometimes it happens in, of all places, the church itself. Do you remember the man who said that he belonged to the church and believed in supporting the church even though he wasn't religious? There is more to his story: A few years later the church undertook its first major building project in a generation. It was a very big project for a small congregation. A month into the project, the chairperson was transferred to another state, and the church turned to this man to take over leadership of the project. He very ably took charge, but in the midst of it, he began to change. He kept noting the seemingly miraculous ways in which God appeared to be making things happen: unexpectedly large gifts during the fund-raising phase, the goodwill of persons who had initially opposed the project, the good weather during the construction phase. When the project was completed, the man asked the pastor for permission to give a report during the sermon one Sunday. He recounted the history of the building project without naming a single human being. His entire report credited Jesus Christ with the success of the project.

This authenticity of faith is not something that we can manufacture, but there are those who have it and the whole church rests on their faith.

That faith is a rock — or as some say, an anvil which has worn out many hammers. As Eastern Europe emerges from nearly a century of communism's official policy of atheism, we are astounded at the survival of a vibrant faith. Many times it was the grandmothers who kept the faith alive. The little old babushkas did not seem very dangerous. They could tell their stories to their little grandchildren, even if they were Bible stories. They could sing while scrubbing the floor, even if they sang hymns. Communism fell to dust and the faith lives on. The great cathedrals in our cities may stand empty but little storefront churches open up a few blocks away. The televangelists may be in jail, but over here is a man, who became sober when he surrendered his life to Jesus, telling a friend that he, too, can overcome his addiction. These people don't worry about someone digging up a parchment scroll proving that Jesus never was. They don't worry about some space satellite launched out to the heart of the universe signaling back that it never ran into God. They don't worry about someone proving that prayer is only a way that the conscious gets in touch with the subconscious. They know Jesus and they know that he is the Christ, the Son of God, and when they die that faith lives on in others. Amen.

---

1. Unpublished Survey on Clergy Morale, Cleveland District of the United Methodist Church Committee on Ministry, 1993.

Proper 17
Pentecost 15
Ordinary Time 22
Matthew 16:21-28 (C)
Matthew 16:21-26 (L)
Matthew 16:21-27 (RC)

Getting Out Of Our Own Way

This is a very dangerous thing to do at the beginning of a sermon, but I'd like to ask you to close your eyes and relax. I realize that means some of you may not reopen your eyes until the benediction! However, I want to take you through a guided meditation.

Close your eyes, sit as comfortably as you can, take a deep breath ... exhale, take another deep breath ... exhale. Now think about the clothes that you are wearing. Think about how your clothes say something about who you are: your gender, your age, your economic status, maybe even how you feel about yourself. As you think about that, imagine yourself in quite different clothes. Note that your real self would not change. Even if you were wearing clothes that we usually associate with the opposite sex or were wearing Eskimo clothes or Arabian clothes, you would still be who you are, so your real self is not your clothes. Therefore, say to yourself, "I am not my clothes."

Think about the place where you live. Think about everything you own. Those things say a lot about you, but are you your possessions? Would you change even if a fire or a flood took everything that you have away? Think about that and say to yourself, "I am not my possessions."

Now think about your job, whether you are a homemaker or work outside of the home or are a student or a retiree. A lot of our identity comes from our job, but if you did something quite different, would your essential self change? Wouldn't you still be you? Think about this and say to yourself, "I am not my job."

Think about your relationships: think about the people who think of you as a friend, or as a brother or sister, or as a cousin, or as a child, or as a parent, or as a spouse. Imagine what it would be like if all these people disappeared from the earth. Would you stop being yourself? Wouldn't your true self persist? Think about this and say, "My relationships are a very important part of my life, but I am not my relationships."

Now become aware of your feelings, both your physical and emotional feelings. You may be in pain at this moment. You may be grieving. Or you may be feeling very peaceful, very happy. Maybe you don't like this exercise and you are irritated and angry or maybe a little frightened. Imagine that somehow the feeling you have at this moment was taken away and an opposite feeling was put in its place. Would you stop being you? Would your essential self really change all that much? Think about this and say, "My feelings are very important, but I am not my feelings."

Pay attention to what you are thinking at this moment. Perhaps you are worried. You are making plans. You are thinking critically about yourself or about me or about people you know. You are thinking about the past or about the future. Obviously our thoughts are very close to our essential selves, yet they are always changing, and something about us never changes. Each of us is always the same person no matter what we are thinking about. Think about this and say, "I am not my thoughts."

Think about your life's experiences. Imagine looking back down the road of life and seeing all the people you have ever known: old friends, old neighbors, old enemies, teachers, schoolmates. See the places you lived, the schools you went to, and the places you worked. Think of funerals and weddings, hospitals, sunsets, dark nights, rainy days and sunny days. Your experiences have done so much to shape you, and yet you have to ask yourself, would I be all that much different if some of my experiences had been different?

Is there something about me that is really me no matter what has or has not happened to me? I have had many experiences, but I am not my experiences.

Who am I? Who am I?

Now, take another deep breath and when you are ready reopen your eyes.

Listen to the words of Jesus again: "If any want to become my followers, let them deny themselves and take up their cross and follow me. For those who want to save their life will lose it, and those who lose their life for my sake will find it."

Some of you just lost your lives — or almost did. Some of you just found yourselves, or almost did.

When someone asks, "Who are you?" what do you answer? Most of us begin with a name, and then — well, it depends who is doing the asking. If I am calling my mechanic to see if my car is done, I'm the owner of a certain kind of car. If I am calling the school to make an appointment with the principal, I am my child's parent. If I am at a family reunion, I am the child of whichever parent it is whose family is having the reunion. If I am calling my doctor to find out about an X-ray, I am a sprained ankle. When I am calling my Congressional representative, I am a voter and a taxpayer. But, if I am talking to God, who am I?

Does God see me only as someone else's brother, or father, or son or husband? Does God see me only as a minister or as an American? Does God's understanding of who I am change when God sees what kind of car I drive or what kind of neighborhood I live in? Does God only think of me as a physical ailment? Does God think of me only as a middle-aged guy whose hair is getting thinner and whose waist is getting thicker?

The person you are before God is that mysterious "I" who isn't what you wear or what you do or what you feel or think or own. Wouldn't you like to find that person — that essential "I"? Don't you sometimes chafe under the false and superficial understandings of yourself that other people have of you — and you too often have of yourself? This so-called "self" that is defined by our jobs, our relationships, our marital status, our social status, our appearance and other externals is really a false self. How do we find the true self — the self that we are before God? To find our selves before God, we have to lose what we think we are or what we think we are supposed to be. Often that feels like crucifixion.

When Jesus went to the cross, he lost everything. He lost his position in the community; instead of being a respected leader, he became a common criminal. He lost his friends and his followers. He lost his only possessions, his clothes, and with them went his dignity. He lost his family. In order to insure his mother's survival, he had to give her away to one of his disciples. There was a terrible moment when he even lost his connection with God: "My God, my God, why have you forsaken me?" Jesus lost everything including life itself, but in losing everything, he became the person he really was before God — the Christ, the son of God.

Listen again to Jesus' words: "If any want to become my followers, let them deny themselves, take up their cross and follow me."

That little exercise we went through at the beginning of this sermon was a denial of our selves. I deny that I am the clothes that I wear. I deny that I am the job that I perform every day. I deny that I am my relationships. I deny that I am my feelings.

In some ways, that exercise is superficial. It's one thing to say to yourself, "Of course I am not my clothes. Of course, I am not my possessions." It is another thing to go and sell all you have and give it to the poor and follow Jesus.

It's one thing to say, "Of course, I am not my job." It's another thing to lose your job or quit your job — or to retire from a job.

It's one thing to say, "I am not my relationships." It is another thing to lose relationships, or to have them change profoundly. Some of you may feel that this morning as you anticipate a child going off to kindergarten. Who will you be if you don't have that preschooler around all day? Some of you have a child going off to college. Who will you be if you have a child who is now an adult? Who will you be if you have an empty nest? You have thought of yourself in a certain way for the last five years or the past 18 years. Now you will be different, because that relationship is different. Even more profound — and much more painful — are the losses caused by death or divorce. Who am I, if I am no longer someone's child? Who am I if I am no longer someone's spouse?

This church is full of people who have suffered losses of possessions, of jobs and of relationships. They know the pain. People who have been through these traumas can tell you, however, that there is something to be discovered when what you always identified as yourself is stripped away. People often find the self that God sees and God knows.

This, however, happens involuntarily and usually painfully. Jesus counsels us to deliberately lose ourselves: "If any want to become my followers, let them deny themselves and take up their cross and follow me. For those who want to save their life will lose it, and those who lose their life for my sake will find it."

This sounds harsh, but it is really a prescription for spiritual health. Letting go of the things that seem to define us gives us the chance to grow and change. I can think of no better place to see the truth of this than a high school class reunion. The healthiest and most interesting and most authentic people at a class reunion are the people who let go of what they were when they were in high school. The most tragic people are the ones who have hung on to the identity they had: the class clown, the jock, the class queen.

Sooner or later many of us come to the conclusion that we need to let go of pieces of our identity and try to find our real selves. When we do that, we will run into difficulty because Satan will stand in our way.

When I speak of Satan, here, I am not talking about Satan as the epitome of evil. I'm speaking of Satan in the same way Jesus was in our gospel lesson. When Jesus says, "Get behind me, Satan," he isn't saying that Peter is the Prince of Darkness. In fact, if it weren't for John Milton and possibly the book of Revelation, we wouldn't even think of Satan as the Prince of Darkness. Satan, throughout most of the Bible, is just the one who keeps getting in people's way. You and I both know, when we are really honest with ourselves, that most people's real problem in life — and our own real problem in life — is that we get in our own way. We are not as loving and as free as we were created to be because we keep getting in our own way.

Sometimes we get in each other's way, too, and we do it thinking that we are being loving. A woman announces to her family that she isn't going to completely define herself as wife and mother anymore. That doesn't mean she stops loving them. It just means that she isn't going to see herself as confined to those two roles anymore. Maybe she is going to get a job or go back to school or become an artist. She wants to find out who she is by letting go of thinking of herself as only a wife and a mother. Her family starts to argue with her. "You can't do that. We need you." They may not actually say it. They may be outwardly supportive, but they begin sabotaging her efforts to do something else with her life. They are getting in her way.

A man starts sharing with his wife that he is thinking of changing careers. Maybe he wants to back off and devote more time to doing volunteer work or to writing a novel. She has some legitimate concerns about paying bills, but maybe some of her identity is tied up with his career. She is the wife of the doctor or the lawyer or the Indian chief. His effort to find himself by losing himself makes her feel like a part of herself is dying, so she begins raising objections and gets in his way.

A son or a daughter comes home from college and announces that he or she wants to be a missionary. Well-meaning parents try to talk some sense into their child. "You could do so much more good by finishing medical school and supporting missionaries with your tithe. You could do community service." What they are really saying is, "I've begun to picture myself as the parent of a certain kind of adult and you are changing my view of myself and of you."

We get in our own way, too. Walter Wink, a Bible scholar, has said that "Satan is yesterday's will of God." When we do the will of God we feel alive; we feel like we are doing the right thing; our lives have meaning and purpose. However, the thing that made us feel alive and which was right for yesterday may not be right today. It may have lost its meaning and its purpose. Remember the class reunion? So often the people who are least likely to change are the ones who enjoyed high school the most — the ones who found meaning and fulfillment in the games, the grades and the goofing off. The ones who are most likely to have let go of their old identities are people like the class nerd, the class drunk, the class slut, and all the ugly ducklings.

It happens later in life, too. We have a tendency to hang on to roles and relationships and even possessions which were right and had meaning at one time in our lives, but have lost that meaning now. It may be the will of God to spend most of one's waking hours looking after a four-year-old, but it may not be appropriate to do that when the child is 14 and it certainly isn't when he or she is 40.

It isn't just our possessions, our careers and our relational roles that get in our way. Our beliefs can also get in our way. We can understand that losing or changing our possessions, our job, our relational roles might help us find the true self, but what about our beliefs? Aren't my beliefs, especially my religious beliefs about God and Jesus Christ, always true and always God's will? Aren't my religious beliefs fundamental to who I am?

No. Our beliefs belong to yesterday. Indeed, our beliefs may even be inherited — even the ones that seem to define who we are.

Many of us are a little like the guy whose friend asked him, "George, are you going to vote for the Democrat in the next election?"

George says, "No, I'm going to vote for the Republican."

His friend says, "Why?"

George says, "Because my father was a Republican and my grandfather was a Republican and my great-grandfather was a Republican — that's why I'm going to vote Republican."

His friend says, "George that's crazy. What if your father was a horse thief and your grandfather was a horse thief and your great-grandfather was a horse thief, what would you be then?"

"Oh," says George, "then I would be a Democrat."

Our beliefs are often inherited. They may have been right and true and meaningful for our parents and grandparents and great-grandparents, but they may get in our way. They may stop us from having an authentic faith in Christ.

That's exactly what happens to Peter in this passage. Only minutes after he affirms that Jesus is the Messiah and Jesus commends him and calls him a rock and tells him he is the foundation of the church, Jesus starts talking about having to die. Now this isn't Peter's understanding of what the Messiah is. Peter had a Sunday school picture of the Messiah in his head. It was a picture of a king who sat on a throne and ruled forever — a king who would never die. He had inherited this belief from his ancestors. He had made it his own, especially as a follower of Jesus, whom he believed to be the Messiah.

He starts to argue with Jesus. "You can't die," said Peter. That's not what the Messiah does. The Messiah lives forever. Peter's most sacred beliefs were getting in the way of his really hearing Jesus and seeing Jesus and understanding Jesus and following Jesus. They were getting in the way of Peter becoming Peter — the disciple or follower of Jesus.

When Jesus says that his followers must be willing to pick up their crosses to follow him and lose their lives in order to find them again, he means that we sometimes have to lose even our beliefs — our faith — so that we can find a truer faith.

Recently a committee interviewed several people who were preparing for the ministry. All of them were second-career people. Each one had lost the life that he or she had been living. Two of them were men in their fifties who had spent most of their lives working as managers in large corporations. Both of them quit their jobs at great financial cost to themselves to go to seminary.

Another was a young woman who had grown up in a very conservative evangelical church. She spoke warmly and movingly of how she had given her life to Christ when she was a teenager and how that meant that Christ needed to become the Lord of her whole life: the way she related to her friends, to her teachers in school, even to her brother. In college, she became part of a group that tried to evangelize other students. As she described her journey, however, something didn't fit the stereotype. She is now a member of a church that is best known for its diverse congregation. It has many interracial couples in the church and recently went on record as a church that openly accepts gays into its membership. She attends a seminary that most people think of as a very "liberal" school.

Someone asked her how she put all of this together in her life. She said, "That was a real crisis for me. I felt, when I gave my life to Jesus, that I had found the truth. How could I find new truth?" The answer to that came to her in understanding that Jesus never changes, but we change in our understanding of him.

Satan is yesterday's will of God. Who are you today? What do you believe today? What must you do today? What do you want today? Sometimes we think of ourselves today as being the person we were yesterday who has the mission that God revealed to us yesterday. That gets in the way of knowing who we are today and knowing what we are called to do today. To take up our cross means that we are willing to let go of everything that was true of us yesterday and let God show us who we are today. We need to die to yesterday in order to be raised up today. That doesn't mean that we don't keep the promises we made. That doesn't mean that there is no consistency in our lives. In fact, the strange thing that we discover is that the more we let go of yesterday, and of who we *think* we are and what we *think* we want, the more consistent we become. There really is a self down there inside of each of us — a self that has been there from the time we were babies and will be there until the day we die. It is that self that Christ calls to follow him over the horizon into a new world. It is that self that needs to let go of everything that isn't itself so that it can pass through the eye of a needle and enter the kingdom of God. Amen.

Proper 18
Pentecost 16
Ordinary Time 23
Matthew 18:15-20

The One Thing That Would Make The Biggest Difference

What one thing could you do that would make the biggest difference in your life and in the world?

Some say praying and reading the Bible every day would make the biggest difference.

Some say working for world peace would make the biggest difference.

Some say doing a kind deed every day would make the biggest difference.

All of these things are important, but I am increasingly convinced that the one thing each of us could do that would make the biggest difference to us and to the world is to rebuild a broken relationship. Nothing would make us pray more or do more to incorporate what the Bible says into the fabric of our lives than taking on the task of rebuilding a broken relationship. Nothing would give our characters more integrity or purpose than rebuilding a broken relationship. Nothing would make us more courageous, more loving, or more fair than rebuilding a broken relationship. Nothing would create more peace in our hearts and minds and in the surrounding world than rebuilding a broken relationship.

Wars and crimes of violence, racial tensions, strikes and political feuds are only the sum total of many interpersonal conflicts: the conflicts between brothers and sisters, parents and children, husbands and wives, neighbor and neighbor. In fact, one of the time-honored methods of reducing conflict in a family or in a nation is to find an outside enemy whom we can all hate together. It only stands to reason then that the rebuilding of any relationship creates a bond of peace and reduces tension and its consequent violence.

Furthermore, when people rebuild broken relationships they learn so much about love and forgiveness and lose so much of their arrogance and self-righteousness and hardness of heart that just their presence in this world creates peace around them.

The church was meant to be the school in which we learn the art of rebuilding relationships.

Heaven knows that there are plenty of schools in which to learn war. Our tax dollars support four military academies and a graduate school called the War College. In fairness, most of the graduates of those schools whom I have been privileged to know are far less combative as individuals than many graduates of business schools, medical schools, law schools, and, I'm sorry to say, divinity schools. The truth is that most of our educational system is based on the polite form of violence we call competition. An environment in which you are graded and evaluated and compared to your peers every day does not teach people how to love one another. Unfortunately, many of our homes are even worse than our school systems when it comes to grading and evaluating and comparing.

I'm not really interested in bashing the military, the schools or our homes. I just want to point out that most of our institutions seem to be set up to create conflict rather than to resolve it.

The Church was meant to be different. The Church was meant to be a community of reconciliation. As Paul wrote to the Corinthians: "All this is from God, who reconciled us to himself through Christ, and has given us the ministry of reconciliation; that is, in Christ God was reconciling the world to himself, not counting their trespasses against them, and entrusting the message of reconciliation to us" (2 Corinthians 5: 18-19).

A ministry of reconciliation means that it is our job to overcome conflicts and rebuild broken relationships.

How do we do that?

First of all, by recognizing that conflict is a fact of life. In general, the church handles conflict the same way it handles that other important fact of life, sex, by pretending it doesn't exist. I suspect that if the church handled conflict better, it would handle sex better, too.

The reason we pretend that conflict doesn't exist is because we don't really believe the gospel is for human beings. We read passages that tell us to "love one another" and to "be of the same mind, having the same love, being in full accord and of one mind" (Philippians 2:2). This passage also tells us that when we are in agreement with one another, God will grant anything we ask. Therefore, we believe that the church should be without conflict. Christian marriages and Christian families should be without conflict.

The truth is, conflict is inevitable. Each of us stands in a different spot and our perspective is different. No one sees the world exactly the same as anyone else. Furthermore, if we are honest with ourselves, we not only see things from our own point of view, but also from the perspective of our own self-interest. When an employer looks at the stub of a paycheck, he or she sees the gross amount and quickly adds in a percentage for health care, vacation time and other benefits. When an employee looks at the stub of a paycheck, he or she sees the net amount after taxes and other deductions and quickly makes other subtractions for the cost of commuting, child care and other unreimbursed, job-related expenses. Conflict between these two points of view are inevitable.

Conflict in families is inevitable. It is inevitable that men and women will see things differently and parents and children will see things differently and a younger child will see things differently than an older child does. No amount of love can erase these differences, not even the passionate love of married people for each other. As James Thurber once wrote: "Marriage is the relationship between one person who cannot sleep with the window open and another who cannot sleep with the window shut."

The being of "one mind" and coming to agreement in prayer that the New Testament speaks of is a miracle that can only take place on the other side of conflict.

We should be grateful to Matthew for recording these common sense instructions on how to resolve conflict.

The first thing we should notice is that the responsibility for resolving any conflict and rebuilding any relationship resides with us. "If another member of the church sins against you, go . . ."

It doesn't say, "Wait for him or her to come to you." It says, "If another member of the church sins against you, go . . ."

It is our responsibility to make things right. No matter who is at fault, it is always our responsibility to take the initiative in rebuilding a relationship. As Matthew records Jesus saying in the Sermon on the Mount: " . . . when you are offering your gift at the altar, if you remember that your brother or sister has something against you, leave your gift there before the altar and go; first be reconciled to your brother or sister, and then come and offer your gift" (Matthew 5:23-24).

If you are like me, you don't take responsibility. If someone has hurt you, you will sit and nurse your grudge until hell freezes over. I mean that metaphor literally. You will be damned if you will go to the trouble and take the risk of seeking out someone who has already hurt you in order to rebuild a relationship with that person. And I mean that figure of speech literally, too. Sartre was wrong. Hell isn't other people. Hell is spending your life — and, maybe eternity — waiting for someone else to make the first move.

It is no accident that Matthew locates these instructions immediately after the parable of the shepherd who leaves 99 sheep in order to go searching for one who is lost. Love always calls us to be the shepherd, to be the one who goes looking for the brother or sister who is lost to us either because we sinned against that person or that person sinned against us.

What does it mean to "sin against someone"? In some ways the argument among English-speaking Christians about the correct way to say the Lord's Prayer teaches us the answer to that question. Some of us say, "Forgive us our trespasses as we forgive those who trespass against us." Others say, "Forgive us our debts, as we forgive our debtors."

Actually both are correct. These instructions about conflict resolution are immediately followed by a parable which illustrates the meaning of forgiveness through a story about the cancellation of real debt. Since that is the text for next Sunday, I will set that aside and concentrate on that other word, "trespasses."

People trespass against us when they do not respect our boundaries. Sometimes that is because neither they nor we are clear about exactly where our boundaries are. Robert Frost once wrote a poem making fun of a neighbor who insisted that "good fences make good neighbors" and that he and Frost were going to repair the stone fence between their two properties even though an apple orchard stood on one side and pine trees stood on the other and, as Frost said, "My apple trees will never get across and eat the cones under his pines." [1]

Frost's neighbor was not entirely wrong, however. It is important for all of us to be clear about where we leave off and other people begin. The first step in making things right with someone who has trespassed against us is to find out where the line between us really is. If we were talking about real property, we could hire a surveyor. In human relationships, we have to make our own survey of where our boundaries are.

That is difficult for some of us. Some people were raised in environments where their boundaries were not respected; where they had no right to privacy or to private thoughts and feelings or to their own opinion. They never had the right to say "no."

When we are not clear about our boundaries, three things seem to be true about us. We take care of people rather than care about them. That often means that we take care of others instead of taking care of ourselves. We are happiest when people say, "I don't know how I would get along without you." We are unhappy when the people we are trying to take care of become unhappy. We redouble our efforts to make them happy and the ungrateful wretches don't appreciate it.

The second thing that happens when we are not clear about our boundaries is that we mistake other people's feelings for our own.

As I just said, we become unhappy when others are unhappy. Some think that is Christian empathy. After all Paul says, "Rejoice with those who rejoice, weep with those who weep" (Romans 12:15). In empathy, however, we knowingly choose to be happy when someone else is happy and to weep when someone else weeps. When we don't know where our boundaries are, we think the other person is *making* us happy or unhappy, angry or peaceful.

The third thing that happens is we lose touch with our own feelings. People who aren't in touch *say* that they are happy when, in fact, they are deeply depressed. They *say* that they love other people when, in fact, they have become angry and bitter.

Frequently, when we become angry with other people, it is because we feel as though they have been taking advantage of us. They have not appreciated us enough. They have little or no concern for our feelings or our limitations. When we feel that way, it is because we have not made our boundaries clear to them and probably not made them clear to ourselves.

The process of going to another person and talking about this can be one of the healthiest things we can do for ourselves. When people use us, we often discover that we have been telling people that it is all right to use us. Many of us fear to confront others with the ways that they have been using us because we are afraid that they will think we are un-Christian — which really means we are afraid that we won't have their approval.

The thing we need to remember is that getting someone's approval is not the point of a healthy relationship. A healthy relationship means sharing life, sharing love. It often means bearing one another's burdens — but notice that means we let others help us just as we help them.

Suppose someone doesn't want a relationship on those terms. Suppose, when we are clear about what our boundaries are, that person pulls away from us, because all that person wants is to use us? "Well, good riddance," we say. Who wants to have a relationship with someone like that?

That's not what the Bible says, however. We are always hearing that we don't need relationships with unhealthy people. That isn't quite right. We don't need unhealthy relationships with unhealthy people. Matthew's gospel tells us not to give up on people as easily as we often do.

If we cannot straighten out a relationship with a one-to-one meeting with another person, or maybe a series of meetings, Jesus tells us to get a couple of other people involved. Many of us want to jump to this stage without going through step one. We want to get other people on our side. Indeed, we would often prefer to complain to someone else and let them handle it, like a child complaining to a parent about a brother or sister.

That is not the purpose of this intervention by others into our relationship with another person. Matthew says that these other people are like witnesses in a court of law. They are to confirm that what you are saying is true.

Why would that be necessary and why would it be helpful in restoring a relationship? Wouldn't it just polarize the relationship even more? Wouldn't it make the person with whom you are trying to rebuild a relationship feel as if you are ganging up on him or her?

Well, it *can* feel that way if your intent is to punish that person rather than rebuild the relationship. However, it can be a very loving thing to do if you believe two things about the other person. One thing is that the other person is not a bad person, and the other is that whatever it is that person is doing that is hurting your relationship is something which he or she doesn't really understand is wrong.

Human nature being what it is, we often resist the truth about ourselves when it requires us to face something we don't want to see, or requires real change on our part. Sometimes we dismiss the observations and even outright complaints of another person. If you are like me, you rationalize that they are just overly sensitive or are upset about something else and are taking it out on me, but when several people confirm that, indeed, I am the one who is being insensitive, I find it harder to rationalize. It forces me to face things in myself that I might not face otherwise.

In fact, this kind of intervention is one of the most effective ways of helping people who are seriously destroying their own lives and the lives of people around them. It is used especially in the treatment of alcoholism and drug abuse in which an addict is surrounded in love by family and friends and coworkers and each person describes what they have seen of that person's addiction and what they have suffered and each person, in turn, asks the "guest of honor" to get help. It is one of the toughest, most emotionally exhausting experiences anyone can go through, but ultimately it is one of the most loving things any group of people can do for someone.

Many people are troubled by the third step in Matthew's gospel, because it has been used by churches through the centuries as a means of excommunication. I don't think we have to be too concerned with it. I think if matters proceeded that far, it would be because, in most cases, we had not been really serious about rebuilding the relationship in stages one and two. In fact, stages one and two probably need to be tried over and over again in order to restore a broken relationship.

However, those who think that this is a formula for excommunication — for consigning someone we love to the outer darkness, have not looked at the context of this passage: not just the fact that this procedure is sandwiched between a parable about searching for a lost sheep and another parable about forgiveness, but also because of the words of Jesus, "If the offender refuses to listen even to the church, let such a one be to you as a Gentile and a tax collector."

Most of the people who were listening to Jesus the day he said that might have taken that to mean that you should have nothing to do with that person ever again, just as the Jews had nothing to do with Gentiles or the despised tax collectors in their own country. One man would have heard those words differently. He would have heard those words just as Jesus meant them. That man was Matthew. Do you remember that, when Jesus called Matthew to follow him, Matthew was a tax collector?

Matthew would have understood from personal experience what Jesus was really saying. Nothing could separate him from the love of Christ and nothing ought to separate us finally from the people we love in Christ. They may choose to go their own way. We may even have to take certain precautions just to protect ourselves physically from some people, but we don't stop loving them even then. And where two or more people agree that even someone who has hurt them deeply can be loved, won't their heavenly father grant anything they ask? Amen.

---

1. Frost, Robert, "Mending Wall" in *Twelve Poets*, Legget, Glenn, ed., (New York: Holt, Rinehart and Winston, 1958) pp. 253-254.

Good News! You Are Going To Be Tortured

Some of you may be familiar with the two-minute radio program, *Ask Dr. Science*. Dr. Science, as the initiated know, isn't a real doctor. He has a master's degree . . . in science!

This disclaimer always runs at the end of the program, however. In the meantime, the announcer asks Dr. Science a question sent in by a listener like, "Why can I only see the stars at night?"

Then Dr. Science answers the question in an annoying know-it-all voice that conveys the unspoken message: "This is a highly complex subject and I am having to condescend to your limited intelligence in order to explain it." His answer, however, always misses the point. "You can only see the stars at night because they have to spend all day putting on their make-up and getting their hair done."

Recently, I have begun to think that I and most of the preachers I know are a lot like Dr. Science when it comes to preaching on the parables of Jesus — especially as they are recorded in Matthew's gospel.

We read these parables and then, as Frederick Buechner says, we explain the life out of them trying so hard "to pound in the point that more often than not all you can hear is the pounding." [1]

I, for one, act as if I know exactly what I am talking about. After all, I'm Dr. Divinity. . . well, I'm not a real doctor. I have a master's degree . . . in divinity! So obviously I am qualified to answer all questions about this passage.

For example, Peter asks Jesus a question a lot of us would like to ask: "How many times should I forgive someone?"

That is a vital question to a lot of people.

How many times do you forgive someone who works for you before you hand him or her a pink slip?

How many times do you forgive someone you work for before you start looking for another job?

How many times do you forgive a friend before you quit making arrangements for lunch?

How many times do you forgive a marriage partner before you walk away from the relationship?

How many times do you forgive a parent or an adult child or a brother or sister before you wash your hands of them?

"How many times should I forgive?" Peter asks. "Seven times?"

Jesus answers, "Not seven times, but, I tell you, 77 times."

Whoops! That's not the way we learned it in Sunday school. It was 70 times 7 back then. Does this New Revised Standard Version of the Bible give us a new revised standard of forgiveness? A leaner, meaner standard for the '90s? Does it mean that the good old days when you could count on someone forgiving you 490 times are over and now you only get forgiven 77 times and then no more Mr. Nice Guy?

Actually, the way the number is written here is ambiguous in Greek. It could be seventy times seven, but scholars say that it is more likely that it means 77. Of course, everybody who ever went to Sunday school or who has sat through a respectable number of sermons knows that it doesn't matter if it is 77 times or 490 times. Jesus is just saying, "Forgive and forgive and forgive." We all nod our heads and say "Amen," and then we leave church and still wonder how many more customers we can afford to lose because of that new salesman before we fire him. We still wonder how many more emotional outbursts from the boss that we will take before we walk. We still wonder how many more times a loved one will come home drunk before we have the locks changed. We still wonder how many more times we can stand being belittled by an in-law before we stay away from family gatherings.

The standard explanation doesn't help much, does it?

Then we put that together with the parable that Jesus tells Peter and get into even deeper water.

As Dr. Divinity, I'm supposed to tell you that this parable is about God's incredible graciousness to us. It surely starts out that way. Jesus says that the kingdom of Heaven can be compared to a king who, in going over his accounts, finds that one of his slaves owes him 10,000 talents which, as we shall see, is a pile of money. The slave promises to work really hard to pay it back. Now, let me play Dr. Divinity and tell you what he is promising. First, figure out what you would be promising if your creditors came to you and said, "You have to pay off your credit card, home equity loan, auto loan and mortgage right now." How many of you could do that? (I'm not asking for a show of hands.)

Suppose you said, "Hey, I don't have that kind of cash lying around but I'll tell you what I'll do. I will pay you every penny of my income until I pay it off. I don't know how I will eat or pay for heat or water or light or my taxes, but I will pay you every penny I make until I pay you everything I owe." A person who owes $45,000 on his house, $4,500 on his car, and $500 on his credit card and who makes $25,000 per year would take two years to pay off that debt, if you don't add on any interest.

At the average daily wage in the time of Jesus, it would take this slave almost 20 years to pay off one talent, and 200,000 years to pay off a debt of 10,0000 talents — and you thought you were over-extended! Even the United States of America isn't that far in debt.

Now the king was touched by this kind of dedication. "I will pay back every penny," the slave promised. Here's a guy who is promising to work overtime, not just for the next couple of week-ends, but for the next couple of ice ages. The king was so moved, that he canceled the debt.

Jesus says the kingdom of heaven may be compared to that king. God has forgiven our debt — a debt we could not pay off in

200,000 years. How many times have we heard that? What difference does it make in our lives?

The slave who has been forgiven this unimaginably huge debt leaves the king's palace and he immediately runs into another slave who owes him the equivalent of about four month's pay. Not a small sum, but certainly much less than the debt he had just been forgiven. He demands payment and his debtor pleads with him in exactly the same words he used with the king. The slave isn't moved by this plea as the king was, and he throws his debtor into prison.

Word of this unmerciful behavior reaches the king, and the king, in anger, uncancels the debt and throws this wretch who had only recently been saved by amazing grace into prison also, and in addition orders that he be tortured until he pays every cent. Remember, this is the guy who, even under the best of circumstances, would have to work for 200,000 years to pay his debt.

That's how the story ends, not in mercy but in vengeance. This is supposed to be a parable of forgiveness, but no one is forgiven. And remember, that king who has just ordered this terrible sentence of thousands of years of suffering is the very one to whom Jesus compares the kingdom of heaven. The kingdom of heaven is not only like a king who forgives a huge debt, but the kingdom of heaven is also like a king who exacts a terrible punishment for the sin of unforgiveness.

Then Jesus, himself, pounds the point home: "So my heavenly Father will also do to every one of you, if you do not forgive your brother or sister from your heart."

I thought this was the gospel — the good news. I don't get it. And that is the truth. I don't get it.

The good news in the Gospel of Matthew, if it is good news, is that nobody "gets it." Do you remember, earlier in the summer, when we heard Jesus tell the parable about the sower who sowed the seeds on the path and the rocks and the good ground, how his disciples asked him, "Jesus, why do you say everything in the form of parables?"

Jesus answered: "The reason I speak to them in parables is that seeing they do not perceive, and hearing they do not listen, nor do they understand" (Matthew 13:13).

We are supposed to hear this parable about the king who forgives a huge debt and then exacts a terrible vengeance as good news. Do you hear it? Do you see it?

What does it take to really understand this parable? A degree in ancient Greek? A good commentary that explains the value of various denominations of ancient Middle Eastern currency? A calculator that can multiply 70 times 7?

No, what it takes to understand this parable is what it takes to understand all the parables. It takes looking into our hearts. What does it mean to forgive from the heart?

There is a simple way for each of us to tell whether or not we have forgiven others. All we have to do is ask if we are free and happy. Are you free to go anywhere and be with anyone? Are you happy — or to use a more Biblical word — do you feel joy?

Some of us will say "yes" too quickly, just as we have said "I forgive you" too quickly. We will say it because we think we are supposed to say it. A good Christian always forgives and a good Christian is happy and free. Some of you are honest enough to say, "No, I'm not really happy, not like the joy I have been led to believe is a gift from God and I'm not really free either. There are some people I can't stand to be around and some people whose eyes I have to avoid. There are some places I cannot go because they contain painful memories." Furthermore, some of you are wise enough to know that this is somehow connected to forgiveness. That wisdom has come out of pain. Sometimes people will sit down with a friend or a counselor or a pastor and admit, "I can't forgive. . ." and that simple confession is the beginning of healing.

I can't forgive. That isn't something most of us find easy to admit unless we can put our finger on some kind of horrible thing that someone did to us — something that most people would say is unforgivable.

A priest wrote in *Sojourners* magazine about little Juanito who lived in an orphanage in San Salvador. He had been found as a small child beneath the bullet-riddled bodies of his mother, grandmother and three older brothers. He struggles to keep his spirits up, but often spends whole days withdrawn, not speaking a word to anyone.

One day after confession, Juanito put his hand on the priest's shoulder and said, "Pray for me, Father, so that I can forgive the soldiers who killed my mother and my brothers. I do not want to live with hatred in my heart." [2]

People like Juanito know that they have to forgive or they will be entombed in the stone-cold prison of bitterness tormented by the fire of rage for the rest of their lives and maybe, who knows, for eternity as well. That very pain will lead them to discover what forgiveness really is.

What about those of us who have not suffered any outrage who are nevertheless imprisoned by our bitterness and tormented by our rage?

Can we admit that we cannot forgive? Can we even say what it is and who it is that we need to forgive? Can we say why we are not happy or do not feel free? John Patton in his book, *Is Human Forgiveness Possible?,* puts forth the idea of the "lost contract." [3] He says that we have contracts with other people. Some of them are explicit, like the marriage vows. We all agree that when someone takes those vows and then is unfaithful to his or her partner, the contract is broken and, in a sense, that person owes a debt to his or her partner.

In Juanito's case, the breaking of the contract is very obvious and everyone would agree that a debt is owed. We have a social contract that we will not take each others' lives. No one could ever pay back Juanito for the loved ones he lost. Nevertheless, the soldiers owe him a debt.

In other cases the contract may be in our hearts. We may not even consciously know that we have such a contract and we might deny it at first, but somewhere deep inside of us is a contract that our parents were always supposed to give us their full attention. A spouse was never supposed to change careers. A child was never supposed to grow up and leave home. "That's silly," we say to ourselves. "That couldn't possibly be why I am unhappy."

We may even have a contract with life. Life is never supposed to be difficult. We are never supposed to grow old. We certainly are not supposed to die.

Again, you might say, "That's silly, no one would think like that." Wait until your doctor tells you that he doesn't like the look of that shadow on the X-ray and you will see how silly it is. You may be surprised at how angry you are at life or at God.

Forgiveness always lies on the other side of finding those hidden contracts — the debts that we have been collecting for our whole lives. I know a man who was secretly angry for 35 years because his mother forgot to make him a cake for his ninth birthday. She owed him a birthday cake and he never got it. He often spoke of that memory in a joking voice that covered deep bitterness and hurt. His mother owed him a debt of 100 denarii and he put her in prison because she could not pay it back. In reality, he was in prison. His bitterness kept him from enjoying life — enjoying his closest relationships. He was tortured by his anger.

Sooner or later we become so unhappy in our prison that we begin to examine our contracts and ask ourselves about these debts. Some are real and they are astronomical and no one is ever going to be able to pay them back.

There are other debts that are not real debts. When we examine our "lost" or secret contracts, we see that we have been expecting other people to be what we are not willing to be and to do what we are not able to do.

There comes a time when a person finally says in his or heart, "Nobody owes me anything." That is what it means to forgive from the heart. It often comes after months, maybe years, of pain. The pain forces us to find a way to end the pain. We finally figure out that the only way to end the pain is to let people off the hook — to cancel their debts. Peace is knowing deep in our hearts that nobody owes us anything. Our families don't owe us anything. Our church doesn't owe us anything. Our employer doesn't owe us anything. Our country doesn't owe us anything. Life itself doesn't owe us anything. When we say deep in our hearts, "Nobody owes me anything," the fires of torment cool and the prison doors swing open and we walk forth as free men and women who know the secret of joy. Amen.

1. Buechner, Frederick, "The Truth of Stories," *Pulpit Digest*, January/February 1992, p. 7.

2. *Sojourners*, April 1989, p. 12

3. Patton, John, *Is Human Forgiveness Possible?: A Pastoral Care Perspective* (Nashville: Abingdon Press, 1985) p. 131 - 136.

Proper 20
Pentecost 18
Ordinary Time 25
Matthew 20:1-16

Good News: Life Is Not Fair

I heard the rooster crow for the third time. I knew dawn was about to break, so I got out of bed and climbed to the roof to where my brother-in-law was sleeping in the cool night air. I tried to rouse him, but he slept on, snoring loudly. The very earliest light illuminated his face as it did my own. I thought about what different men the sunlight was falling on. I couldn't remember a day in my life — except for sabbaths — when I slept past dawn. I doubt my brother-in-law had ever seen the dawn, unless it was through the bleary eyes of a man just going to bed after partying all night.

I had told him the night before that the harvest would be at its peak this morning and I expected him to get up with me and see if we could both get hired to work in the fields. It was the one day of the year when there was more work than there were people to do it, and even my brother-in-law could get a job. He started to complain about his back, but I glared at him and he shut up. I'll give my wife credit. She backed me up. She told the lazy good-for-nothing to do what I said.

But here he was, dead to the world. I didn't have time to wake him and wait for him to get dressed and come with me. I'd let my wife sort that out later. I climbed down the ladder and walked down the street to the center of town. I was irritated to see that one or two others had arrived before I did. I liked to be the first man there every morning. I was known as the hardest worker in the town. I cursed my brother-in-law for delaying me. It didn't really matter. The landowners had not arrived yet. I was surprised, however, that one did come hurrying in just as a couple of other men arrived. I pushed myself to the front of the group, but didn't need to. He asked us all if we wanted to work. He needed all of us. I told him that we would work if he paid each of us one denarius for a day's wage. That was usual, so he agreed and we went with him.

The dew had burned off as we bent over the stalks of grain, swinging our scythes and binding our sheaves. We were not unhappy when, a couple of hours later, the landowner left and returned with some more harvesters to help us. I noticed, however, that my brother-in-law was not among them.

The sun rose to its zenith and we broke for the midday meal. More harvesters joined us and we worked slowly through the hot afternoon, but the field was far from done. The sun now is low in the sky and we see the worried landowner leave again and soon he returns with more people. My brother-in-law is among them. I wonder where the landowner found them. They are the ones who have never done an honest day's work in their lives. I watch out of the corner of my eye as the landowner hands them harvesting knives and they take them uneasily into their hands. I see them walking warily out into the field. They look around trying to figure out what they are supposed to do. My brother-in-law watches me for a moment as I swing my knife and cut a swath of grain — the stalks fall smoothly all in one direction. He tries to swing his harvest knife the way I am doing it. He's at the wrong angle though. The knife twists and falls out of his hand. He picks up his knife and tries it again. This time he hits too high on the stalk. The grains shake loose and fall to the ground, of use only to the widows and orphans who will descend upon the field at nightfall to pick up the smallest grains from the ground. Although there is little use in it, my brother-in-law begins chopping at the base of the stalks of grain like a woodsman cutting a tree with an axe. While I carefully gather my bundle of grain in my arms to tie it into a sheaf, he is faced with stalks which have fallen every which way, like a child's game of pick-up-sticks. It will take him what's left of the daylight to pick up that mess and tie it up, all for only a handful of grain.

I move on shaking my head. How do such people survive? I wonder. Of course, I know how my brother-in-law survives. When we were boys, we were in the synagogue school together. He always tried to copy my letters. Whenever he was called upon to read from the scriptures he complained of a sore throat. I knew the rabbi didn't believe him, but the boy knew so little that it pained the rabbi to hear him try to read the holy book. Nevertheless, I often heard the rabbi praise the boy's work to his mother. I think the rabbi felt sorry for her. Her husband drank too much wine and her life was hard. I was no scholar, but I tried. I did my best. I got what I deserved — no more and no less.

For most of his life, my brother-in-law survived because his mother fed him and provided him with a home. When his mother died, his sister — my wife — took him in. I was ashamed of my brother-in-law, but my wife has borne me so many sons, I say nothing. I often think, however, about how fortunate I was to learn the hard lessons of life early. No one took care of me when I was old enough to work. I had to earn my way before I was fully grown. The toughness of life made me a man who asks for nothing except a fair day's wage for a fair day's work.

Finally, the fields were cleared. The sheaves were set up on the threshing floor. There would be work tomorrow for those willing to beat the heads of grain off the stalks and and throw the straws in the air to be carried off in the breeze. I would be there. I doubt the landowner would hire my brother-in-law, though, no matter how shorthanded he was. I saw the landowner eyeing the one sheaf of grain my brother-in-law managed to tie together.

The landowner told the foreman to line us up in the order we had been hired. This was usual and so I went to the front where I always did. The foreman knew me and said, "Not today, Avram. He wants the last hired to be first."

Probably wants to chew them out and send them off with nothing, I thought. So I shrugged and went to the end of the line. I resented this little game. I had been on my feet all day and I wanted to be paid and go home.

The landowner called his steward, who was carrying a bag of money. The steward told those in front to step forward one-by-one and pressed a coin into each one's hand. I assumed it might be a penny or two. I didn't pay much attention, until my brother-in-law stepped forward, received his pay and then let out a whoop and ran to the back of the line and said, "See, Avram, a whole denarius!"

I think it was the first time anyone had ever paid him a day's wage in his life. Too bad he hadn't earned it. I assumed the landowner was desperate and the last bunch he had hired had driven a hard bargain, but my brother-in-law said they hadn't haggled at all. The landowner hadn't promised to pay them at all. He just invited them to work in the fields. "Nobody ever hired me before, Avram!" he said.

His gratitude to the landowner was touching — and well-deserved. The landowner certainly hadn't gotten much in exchange for his denarius.

My mood lightened, too. I figured the landowner was in a good mood. He was inclined to be generous and, if he was fair, I ought to make about 10 times as much as my brother-in-law. So, when the steward called my name, I didn't just hold out an empty palm to receive a coin, because I expected the steward would pour out much of what was left in the bag. But no! The steward took out only one denarius and dropped it into my cupped hands.

"What is this?" I asked the steward.

"It is your pay," he said.

"But I worked all day!" I cried.

The landowner heard me and came over and asked what was wrong.

I told him that I and the men who were left had worked since dawn and we were being paid only one denarius.

"Isn't that what we agreed to?" asked the landowner. I admitted it was, but I said it was not fair that the men who had worked all day in the heat of the sun should be paid the same as those who only dawdled for an hour in the cool of the evening.

The landowner asked me whose land I had worked on. I told him it was his. He pointed to his bag of money and asked who it belonged to. I admitted that it belonged to him. "If I want to be generous, I will be generous," he said. "Now take your pay and leave."

So I did. I smoldered as I walked down the road listening to my brother-in-law laughing and thanking God for having received a whole denarius. To add to my mood, it began to rain gently. My brother-in-law raised up his arms and thanked God for the rain, talking about how refreshing it was, how cool it felt after all that work.

"All that work!" He had hardly broken a sweat. The rain only made me steam like a hot rock.

Finally, my brother-in-law noticed my mood and quieted down. He asked me why I was angry.

I said, "Because I have to put up with a fool like you, because I have a wife and five sons and I not only have to feed them but I have to put food in your useless mouth as well, because I got up before dawn this morning and worked all day for the same pay that you got, because I am going to work hard all my life and you are going to play all your life and when we get done, our bodies will be rolled into the same hole in the ground." While I was talking, the rain came down harder. It was running in our eyes. It was rolling off our ears. Our hair and clothes were sopping wet.

Suddenly, I saw myself and heard myself as if I were another person. I saw my face covered with rain as if I had been crying all my life. I heard my mournful voice talking about my body being rolled into a hole in the ground. I began to laugh.

My brother-in-law looked at me in astonishment. "Avram," he said finally, "I've never heard you laugh before."

I considered this for a moment. He was right. Oh, I had laughed with a fatherly "ho-ho-ho" when one of my children did something that pleased me. I had come close to real laughter on my wedding day, but I didn't want to be even more the butt of my groomsmen's jokes than I already was. I had laughed with derision when I saw my brother-in-law trying to cut wheat; but I had never laughed freely, joyously — for no reason. I could understand my brother-in-law's consternation. Here I was the most serious, uncompromising, rigid and, yes, angry person he knew, laughing my head off while standing soaking wet in the rain.

"What's so funny?" he asked.

"You," I said. "Me. Look at us. Did you ever see such different people?" My brother-in-law looked at me closely.

"No," he said. "No two men could be more different from each other than you and I are, Avram. You are always up at the crack of dawn. I sleep all morning. You work hard all day. I don't even know how to work. My sister loves you. People look at me with contempt. You have five strong sons. I have no one."

"Not true," I said. "That's not entirely true, brother. My family is yours as well."

"Avram," my brother-in-law asked, "have you lost your mind?"

"Maybe," I laughed, "but I think I have found my soul. Look at us, brother. Two men so different, yet look at the same rain falling on us both. And didn't the same sun warm our backs today? Mine bent over in the field and yours curled up in a blanket on the roof."

"I still don't understand," he said. "What does the sun and the rain have to do with it?" By this time the rain was letting up and the sky was clearing in the west.

"Tell me, again, brother," I asked. "What did the landowner tell you he was going to give you if you would come to work for him for that last hour?"

"He didn't promise us anything," my brother-in-law said. "He just asked us if we would come and work for him."

"And you didn't bargain with him?" I asked. "None of your friends said to the landowner, 'what's it worth to you' or 'what do we get out of it?' "

He shook his head, "I guess we were so surprised to be asked to work, we didn't even think about what we would get paid."

I laughed. "That's the way you have lived your life," I said. "And this morning I bargained to work for a whole day for one denarius, because that is the way I have lived my whole life. My whole life is a bargain. Everything is supposed to be a fair exchange. Your sister bore me five sons, so I put up with you. I work harder than any other man in town and I should get paid first. I am honest and keep the sabbath and honor my father and mother and so God should bless me and I should go to heaven."

"Yes, Avram," said my brother-in-law, "and I and my friends will go to the place of torment."

"Really?" I said with mock interest. "Tell me about this place of torment."

My brother-in-law didn't understand that I was joking because he answered seriously: "It is a terrible place — like the town garbage dump, where the fire burns forever and people like me are eaten by worms. Some say it is on the other side of a bottomless canyon from heaven. Others say that heaven is a beautiful city and hell is a lake of fire outside the city gates."

"So, if I go to heaven," I said, "I can watch you burning in this lake of fire?"

My brother-in-law said seriously, "The teachers say that part of the joy of heaven is seeing the sufferings of the unfaithful."

"In other words," I said, "there wouldn't be any fun in going to heaven if nobody went to hell."

My brother-in-law looked at me cautiously. "What are you saying, Avram?"

"I'm saying, where is this God?" I replied. "Where is this God who sorts out everyone so fairly and rewards some and punishes others? Do you see a God like that anywhere in this world, brother? Do you see fairness all around you? Is the sunshine fair? Does it only shine on the good people while the bad walk in darkness? Is the rain fair? Does it just water the believer's garden and stop at the fence of the unbeliever? Is death fair? Do only bad people die?"

My brother-in-law only blinked at me. The answer to these questions was so obvious.

"Who sends the sunshine and the rain, brother?" I asked. "Who decides when we shall live and when we shall die?"

Again, my brother-in-law blinked at me, because the answer was obvious.

"God is like the landowner," I said. By this time the setting sun had broken through the clouds and in the east we saw one of the brightest rainbows I ever saw in my life.

"But, Avram," my brother-in-law protested, "the landowner wasn't fair. He wasn't just. God is a God of justice."

"How did you feel," I asked, "when the landowner gave you a denarius for your work?"

My brother-in-law thought for a moment. "I felt like I didn't deserve it, but I was very grateful. It was more than I dreamed of receiving. I . . . I felt happy," he said finally.

"That's how I feel about that rainbow," I said. "And I never felt that way about a rainbow before. I'm not sure I ever really looked at one before. Can you see it, brother?" I asked.

"Of course I can see it, Avram," he said.

"Well, I'm astonished and angry," I said with a laugh. "A lazy good-for-nothing like you shouldn't be able to see that beautiful rainbow. That should only be for us good people. Why should you get to see it? You didn't earn it."

"You didn't earn it either, Avram," he said angrily. He didn't get the joke.

"Of course, I didn't earn it, brother," I said. "No one earns the right to see a rainbow. No one earns the right to be loved. No one earns the right to have a child. No one earns the sunshine and the rain. I'm not even sure I earned this denarius," I said, tossing the coin in the air and catching it. "I only know that having it means that we will have bread on the table tomorrow. After that, I'll have to trust in God to take care of me, the way you trust me to take care of you."

"But, Avram," he said, "I think I know what you are talking about now. If people don't think they can earn things, why would they work?"

"Because they like to," I said. "Heaven knows, I must like to, I do enough of it."

"I liked it, too, Avram. It felt good to be in the fields with the others. I've always envied you having someplace to go — having a purpose."

"Sometimes it's too much of a purpose," I said. "Other things are important, too."

"Avram," my brother-in-law said, "if I went with you tomorrow to the threshing floor, would you show me how to do the things you know how to do?"

"Sure," I said.

"Great!" he said excitedly. "I'll be up before dawn."

"Well," I said, "you may have to wait. Tomorrow morning, I want to sleep in."

Proper 21
Pentecost 19
Ordinary Time 26
Matthew 21:23-32 (C)
Matthew 21:28-32 (L, RC)

It's Your Funeral

Today people in our society are less and less willing to completely leave things to the "experts." Patients insist that their doctors talk to them about the options for treatment and include the patient as a full partner in making the final decision. The computer software stores are full of programs that allow people to draft simple legal documents like wills and to keep financial records and fill out tax forms like an accountant. People are saying to doctors, "It's my body." They are saying to lawyers and accountants, "It's my business and my future." They are saying to auto mechanics, "It's my car." Couples who want to get married say to me, "It's our wedding." Very few people say, "It's my funeral."

Why am I talking about all of this today? So that I can give you a piece of advice and preach a short sermon.

First, the advice. It's nothing you haven't heard before. Do your next-of-kin a favor and write down your wishes for your funeral service. Don't, whatever you do, tell them not to have a funeral. I'm sorry to inform you of this; it may be your funeral but your funeral is not for you; it's for the people who love you. If they think they don't need some formal way to say good-bye, then let them decide that. Otherwise, at least give them the option of spending half an hour worshiping God while surrounded by the people who love them. However, in planning that funeral, it would probably help them to worship and to be healed if they knew your favorite hymns and your favorite Bible passages. You might even write something to be read to your loved ones at the funeral. Some people even make audiotape or videotape messages.

That's my advice. Now here is the sermon. This sermon revolves around planning a funeral for someone else.

When I sit down with a family to plan a funeral for someone who has died, I may ask if they have any particular passages from the Bible that they want included in the service. If it is to be held in the church, I may ask about hymns they would like played or sung. The most difficult task, however, is determining what to say about the person who has died. No one pretends that we can adequately sum up a person's life in five or ten minutes. However, it is helpful to understand the purpose of the words at a funeral. Some funeral services divide what we usually call the "sermon" into three parts: the Naming, the Witness, and the Sermon.   The Naming usually includes the kind of information you might put on a resume or into a biography: when and where the deceased was born; the name of his or her spouse and the names of any children; jobs that person held and places the person called "home"; the person's hobbies and membership in organizations; and maybe a word about the circumstances of his or her death. The Witness is more personal. We may speak of the deceased's courage or love or sense of humor or friendship or sense of responsibility or contributions to the community. In the sermon, we would speak about the promise of eternal life and the promise that those who mourn shall be comforted. These three sections can be divided among three speakers; perhaps a partner or a coworker could do the "naming" — talk about the public life of the deceased; a close friend or family member could bear witness to the private life; and the family's pastor could preach a sermon. I usually offer families this option. In practice, however, even people who are accustomed to public speaking find it difficult to speak when their grief is fresh and sharp. I often read the speech someone else has written but cannot find the voice to say. Usually the family just asks me to say something so I weave the naming, witness and sermon into one.

How do we "name" someone — tell who that person is — in a way that is both honest and personal? And how do we witness to the grace of God in someone's life — again, in an honest way?

The words that are spoken at a Christian funeral, whether we call them a sermon, a naming, or a witness cannot be characterized as a eulogy. A eulogy praises a person who has died. In Christian worship, we praise God, not people. That does not keep us from saying good things about the deceased. It does mean that we see the grace of God in a person's life and it is the business of a funeral sermon to point out that grace.

I think it is important to say that, because a lot of people hate eulogies at funerals, and rightly so. Not many of them are honest. In fact, one of my nightmares is to miss the mark as widely as the poor preacher did at a funeral for a relative of a friend of mine. She said the minister went on about what a cheerful man cousin Dan was — how he always had a smile on his face. Most of those assembled must have wondered about whom he was talking. After all, my friend said, she learned the meaning of the word "curmudgeon" when she looked it up in the dictionary and saw a picture of Dan's face.

How do we witness to the grace of God honestly and without judgment at a funeral? By remembering that at every funeral we are probably burying one or the other of the two sons in this parable.

Some people apparently said "no" to their heavenly Father all of their lives. They certainly said "no" to the church. They never went. Some of them were even contemptuous of what they called "organized religion." (Which only shows how little they ever knew about it. If you ever find an organized religion, please let me know, I'd like to join.) Some even said "no" to Jesus Christ. There are some preachers who say that such people don't deserve a Christian burial. My feeling is that whether a burial is Christian or not Christian depends more on the people who are doing the burying than on the person being buried.

That is precisely the position you may find yourself in someday. You may have to bury someone close to you who has been a proud pagan. What do you do?

In some cases, Paul can help us out: "For it is not the hearers of the law who are righteous in God's sight, but the doers of the law who will be justified" (Romans 2:13).

In other words, there are many who have not professed the Christian faith who practiced it. They are like the son who said to his father that he wouldn't go to work in the vineyard and then went anyway.

There are, of course, those who not only didn't profess the Christian faith, but who did not live exemplary lives either. Some people make rather spectacular failures of their lives. Yet, there is always something that one can say about the grace of God in a person's life. Indeed, if you look hard enough, the spectacular failures have sometimes done some spectacularly good things. I think, for example, of a story told me by an old retired minister when I was preparing for the ministry.

He graduated from seminary just before World War I and he was appointed to a church in a very small town. He had been there only a couple of weeks when he received the call every new minister dreads — the call to do his first funeral. The person who had died was not a member of his church. She was, in fact, a woman with a very bad reputation. Her husband was a railroad engineer who was away from home much of the time. She had rented rooms in their house to men who worked on the railroad and rumor had it that she rented more than just rooms when her husband was away. The young preacher, faced with his first funeral, found no one who had a good word to say about this woman, until he entered the small old-fashioned grocery store on the day before the funeral. He began to talk to the store owner about his sadness that the first person he would bury would be someone about which nothing good could be said. The store owner didn't reply at first and then, in his silence, he appeared to make a decision. He took out his store ledger and laid it on the counter between him and the preacher. He opened the ledger at random and, covering the names in the left-hand column, he pointed to grocery bills written in red — groceries that people had bought on credit — and then the column that showed the bill had been paid.

He said, "Every month, that woman would come in and ask me who was behind in their grocery bills. It was usually some family who had sickness or death — or some poor woman trying to feed her kids when her husband drank up the money. She would pay their bill and she made me swear never to tell. But, I figure now that she is dead, people ought to know — especially those who benefited from her charity who have been most critical of her."

"Truly I tell you, the tax collectors and the prostitutes are going into the kingdom of God ahead of you."

If you look hard enough, you can find good in just about anyone. I say "just about" because I'll leave open the possibility that someone's life may be completely devoid of good, but I haven't found that person yet.

I have come close on occasion. The saddest cases are those who haven't been great sinners or saints — but whose lives were just mediocre. I sometimes think about how, in the book of Revelation, the Spirit of Christ condemns the church in Laodicea because they "are neither cold nor hot." Lukewarmness — mediocrity — makes Jesus gag (Revelation 3:14-16).

Yet even these people always have good intentions. I remember one of the first funerals I did. I tried to follow the old preacher's example and find something good about the woman who had died. I asked nearly everyone. No one, including her own son, had anything good to say about her. They didn't have anything bad to say, either. It was just as if she had not lived. To some extent this is the fault of the people closest to the person who has died. They just haven't paid attention. I am well aware that more than half the stories I hear from people before a funeral are more about the person telling the story than they are about the deceased.

I sat in the woman's living room talking to her son, and noticed a poem in a frame on the wall. It was a familiar poem about wanting to live in a house on the side of the road and to be a friend to the human race. I asked the son about the poem and he said it was his mother's favorite. That was what she had wanted to do with her life. As I heard the cars whizzing past on the highway outside the front door, I knew that she had chosen to fulfill at least part of that ideal — she did, indeed, live in a house on the side of the road.

So, in that funeral sermon, I talked not so much about who the woman was as about what she wanted to be.

Is that such faint praise that it damns the person just as effectively as saying, "Here was a totally wasted life"? Isn't saying that "so-and-so wanted to be a better person than he or she was but didn't have the moral courage to live it," just saying that this person is like the son in the parable who said he would go to work in the vineyard and didn't?

Yes, it is.

Well, isn't this parable a condemnation of people like that? Doesn't Jesus ask us, "Who did the father's will? The son who said he wouldn't work and then did it anyway or the son who said he would and didn't?" And isn't the answer obvious?

Yes, the son who said he wouldn't work and did it anyway did the father's will and the one who said he would go and didn't did not do the father's will, but to say this parable condemns that second son is reading too much into it.

In the first place, note that this parable is about two sons. Jesus only tells two parables about a father who has two *sons*. The other is the parable of the prodigal son. He tells several parables about a vineyard. We heard one last week about the workers who were all paid the same regardless of how long they worked. The very next passage is another parable about servants in a vineyard. This, however, is not a parable about workers or servants, but about a parent and his children.

If you hired someone to do a certain job and he said he would do it and didn't, you probably would fire him. If you told your son or daughter to do something and he or she agreed but didn't do it, you would not fire your own child. You can't.

Notice, Jesus doesn't say what happened to the two sons. If he had wanted to condemn the second son, Jesus might have concluded with him being tortured, like the unforgiving servant. The parable just ends. It is left to us to imagine what the father did with these two sons.

That, my friends, is exactly the position we are in at a funeral. We know two things when someone dies. The first is: This is a child of God. The second is: All of God's children are loved equally well. There is one big thing that we do not know. We don't know what the Heavenly Parent does with a child who has disobeyed God's will. Nor do we know what the Heavenly Parent does with a child who has insulted God.

If we heard this parable with Middle Eastern ears, we would be shocked and scandalized by the first son's outright refusal to obey his father. This is not a typical American household where it is common for a father to say to his son, "Hey, Kid! You goin' to take out the garbage like your mother askt 'cha or what?"

And the son, watching MTV, shouts back, "Hey! get off my back! I'm busy, okay?"

If that scene is familiar you may want to write down the reference for this passage:

> *If someone has a stubborn and rebellious son who will not obey his father and mother, who does not heed them when they discipline him, then his father and his mother shall take hold of him and bring him out to the elders of his town at the gate of that place. They shall say to the elders of his town, "This son of ours is stubborn and rebellious. He will not obey us. He is a glutton and a drunkard." Then all the men of the town shall stone him to death. So you shall purge the evil from your midst; and all Israel will hear, and be afraid* (Deuteronomy 21:18-21).

The point is, sons did not tell their fathers that they weren't going to work in the fields. The father would be disgraced by such behavior. The first son is not blameless in this story.

Neither son is blameless in this story. That is the way it is in our relationship to God. That is true even when we look at the lives of great saints. Everyone has feet of clay. Martin Luther was a man who needed enemies like other men need friends. John Wesley was an utter failure as a husband.

Almost always, when I do a funeral for a man or woman who has been a pillar of the church, I can see people in the congregation who have ambivalent feelings at this person's passing. Often, they are sitting in the front row. It can sometimes be a terrible burden to be married to or to be the child of a very good man or woman. Sometimes their greatest virtues can be the biggest burden we can bear.

A friend of mine told me of the recent passing of his grandmother at the age of 96. The little church where she had worshipped for most of her very long life was full of people. Maybe a third of them were family. The rest were people who had known her as their Sunday school teacher, their neighbor, their friend. They knew her as the woman who ran the rummage sales and who counted the offering every Sunday. She was always there at that little church, just as she had always been there for her children and her grandchildren.

My friend said that when he visited her in the nursing home, she had been telling one of her nurses about some of her 20 great-grandchildren. The nurse wondered how she could remember all their names. His grandmother said, "Because I pray for them every day."

My friend, who is a minister, did not preach the sermon at that funeral. That was the job of his grandmother's pastor, who also was his parents' pastor. He did say the prayer of thanksgiving at the end. He prayed about how much his grandmother had loved all of her family and friends and then briefly acknowledged that that love sometimes held on too tightly. In that moment, he said something that needed to be said. His grandmother's children and grandchildren had sometimes felt that they couldn't pursue some of their dreams because to do so would have meant leaving this loving person behind and they didn't want to hurt her.

It's all right to tell the truth at a funeral, as long as we tell it gently. No one is perfect. Indeed, we are all far from being perfect. We all live contradictory lives. Some folks seem cold and selfish on the outside, and hide their great passion and love in such a way that it only emerges in secrecy or in their dreams. Others of us make public professions of faith and try to build reputations as people who are faithful to God, but we fail to live up to our ideals in some very important areas of our lives.

Yet, we are all children of God. Someday, someone you know very well will die. I hope that whoever is in charge of the service will ask your help in preparing it and will ask you specifically what you would like said about this person. You can be loving and you can be honest at the same time. You can find the good in the worst life. You can find high aspirations in the most wasted life. You can admit the faults of the most exemplary life and celebrate the grace of God in every life, because we are all children of God. Those who outwardly reject God and secretly obey, as well as those who profess faith in God and desire to please God and fail to live by that faith or to do God's will, are all children of God. It is not for us to judge. It is for us to look at those lives, love them, learn from them and then live our own lives by God's grace as well, knowing that God accepts us, just as we are. Amen.

Proper 22
Pentecost 20
Ordinary Time 27
Matthew 21:33-46 (C)
Matthew 21:33-43 (L, RC)

Why Do We Ignore Warning Signs?

Recently the *New York Times Magazine* showed a series of photographs of a rock formation in Yosemite National Park near Bridal Veil Falls. A prominent sign in yellow plastic was attached to the rocks which clearly said: "Danger. Climbing or scrambling on rocks and cliffs is extremely dangerous. They are slippery when dry or wet. Many injuries and even fatalities have occurred." One picture showed a woman walking on the rocks in a tight dress and high heels. Another showed a couple walking on the rocks. The man was carrying his dog apparently because he thought it was too slippery for the dog. Another showed a man carrying a month-old baby in his arms while walking on the rocks.[1]

What is it about people that causes us to ignore clear warnings? Why do folks rip the plastic cover off a pack of cigarettes when all of us know the surgeon general's warning by heart? Why do people remove the safety shield from power saws? Why do people ignore their doctor's warnings about being overweight and underexercised? Why do entire civilizations ignore warnings about pollution or the revolutionary pressures that economic and political injustice creates?

In some ways, the whole Bible could be characterized as a book about how God gives the human race warnings and we ignore them.

God warns Adam and Eve not to eat the fruit of the tree of the knowledge of good and evil or they will die. God gives Noah the plans for a boat that takes him more than a century to build — time enough, surely, for his neighbors to get the message that a flood was coming. Moses tells Pharaoh to let the Hebrew people go or God will visit plagues upon Egypt and, even when the plagues start coming, Pharaoh refuses to listen. The prophets tell Israel to change its ways or suffer the consequences, but Israel ignores the prophets, beats them, even kills some of them — and suffers the consequences of invasion, slavery and exile.

Jesus warns the religious leaders in the parable we just read. It was a parable that Jesus told on the Monday after Palm Sunday. The religious leaders had challenged his right to preach in the temple in Jerusalem. The parable is an allegory. The vineyard is both the land of Israel and also the religion of Judaism. The tenants are the religious leaders. God is the landowner who sends servants to the religious leaders to tell them to pay their rent — that is, to acknowledge God as Lord. The religious leaders have ignored, persecuted and even killed these servants whom we call the prophets. Finally, the landowner sends his son, whom we understand to be Jesus, the Son of God. Jesus knows that these religious leaders have already decided to kill him, so he builds that into the parable. Then he asks the religious leaders, "What will the landowner do to these tenants who have driven away his servants, the prophets, and killed his son?"

The religious leaders give the obvious answer: the landowner will come in and kill the tenants.

Oddly, Jesus is not quite so bloodthirsty. He does say, however, that they will be displaced by others.

The parable is a warning — the last warning the religious leaders will get. Had they listened to it, all of history would have been changed. There would have been no cross. We do not know what God would have done. From Matthew's point of view, the religious leaders' decision to execute Jesus was inevitable. From the very beginning Jesus said, "For this people's heart has grown dull, and their ears are hard of hearing, and they have shut their eyes; so that they might not look with their eyes, and listen with their ears, and understand with their heart and turn — and I would heal them" (Matthew 13:15).

Nevertheless, Jesus keeps trying to get through to them, to warn them, to get them to turn their lives around so that he can heal them.

What is it about people anyway? Why do we ignore warnings?

The answer is that we are afraid.

It sounds crazy. You would think that fearful people would jump when they heard a warning, but that is not true. Fearful people construct false beliefs to protect them from their fears. We know what some of those false beliefs are: the belief that we are immortal, that we are exceptions to the rule; the belief that one more drink, one more cigarette, one more cheeseburger, one more step out on to the ledge won't hurt us; the belief that those who are making the warnings don't know what they are talking about or they are exaggerating the danger. For example, in the early 1800s, Thomas Malthus predicted that the rapid growth of earth's human population would cause mass starvation and the end of civilization before 1950. Those kind of predictions make us take all warnings with a grain of salt.

We believe that we are somehow in control. In Tom Wolfe's book about the first astronauts, *The Right Stuff*, he says that the corps of young test pilots from which the first astronauts were drawn spent a lot of time going to the funerals of comrades who were killed in the planes they were testing. Going home from those funerals, they didn't face the reality that testing experimental aircraft is an inherently dangerous line of work. Rather, they told themselves that the difference between themselves and the man they had just buried was that they had the right stuff and he didn't. So also, we tell ourselves: Why should I fasten my seat belt? I haven't even scraped a bumper in 20 years. What are the chances that I am going to be in a car accident this afternoon?

We understand these psychological tricks we play on ourselves. Well, let me put it this way: we understand these psychological tricks other people play on themselves. We seldom understand the psychological tricks we play on *our*selves — if we did, we wouldn't play them.

The Bible, however, is more concerned with the *theo*-logical trick we play on ourselves. Jesus describes it in the tenth chapter of Matthew where he says, "Do not fear those who kill the body but cannot kill the soul; rather fear him who can destroy both soul and body in hell" (Matthew 10:28).

The theological trick we play on ourselves is to fear the wrong thing, the wrong people, the wrong situations. The tenants in the parable were afraid of paying the rent. They should have been afraid of the landowner. The religious leaders were afraid of losing their power. They should have been afraid of killing the Messiah.

As I read this passage, I thought about how Jesus' situation here is like that of so many other seemingly powerless people threatened by those who have a great deal of power. I imagined a human rights worker in a country like Guatamala surrounded by secret police in the basement of some secret prison. The human rights activist could warn the secret police that harming her would cause world opinion to turn against their government. The secret police would probably laugh. They aren't afraid of world opinion. They are afraid of revolution. They are afraid of losing power. They are afraid that if they don't harshly oppress the poor people of their country, their own families and the families of those who hire them will suffer. They also do not quaver with fear when they hear the prophecy of Martin Luther King, Jr., who said, "The arc of history is a long, long arc, but it bends toward justice."

Scholars are not sure exactly when in the first century A.D. Matthew wrote his gospel, but the theories tend to converge on a time right before or right after the Romans attacked and destroyed Jerusalem in the year 70 A.D. It was a period of incredible suffering for the Jews, and Matthew may have seen it as the judgment of God upon the Jews for having rejected and crucified Jesus. He may have seen it as a literal fulfillment of the prophecy that the landowner "will put those wretches to a miserable death, and lease the vineyard to other tenants who will give him the produce at the harvest time." However, most of those who suffered would have been small children or were not even born when Jesus died on the cross.

It is true that the arc of history bends toward justice. It is true that the crimes of a Hitler or a Stalin or of a military dictatorship in Chile or Argentina are eventually brought to light. However, the individuals who perpetrated the crimes are often not punished. Unless, of course, they go to hell.

When Jesus speaks of killing the body and soul in hell, however, he isn't talking about the hell of fire so vivid in popular imagination. He is simply talking about death. He is talking about spiritual death. I don't know what happens to us after death, but I do know it is possible to kill your own soul in this life. We kill our souls when we refuse to pay the rent on life.

What is the rent Life with a capital *L* demands? An ancient prophet wondered about this. Given the value of life, one might expect that the rent would be stupendous: "Will the LORD be pleased with thousands of rams, with ten thousands of rivers of oil?" (Micah 6:7). Then, however, the prophet tells us what the rent really is, "He has told you, O mortal, what is good; and what does the LORD require of you but to do justice, and to love kindness, and to walk humbly with your God?" (Micah 6:8).

Justice, *kindness*, and *walking humbly* are just about the biggest words in the Old Testament. *Justice*, in the Bible, means something more than just having the punishment fit the crime or a fair distribution of scarce resources. It means the establishment and preservation and rebuilding of a right relationship. It means that I live with my neighbor in such a way that I can look her in the eye and she can look me in the eye. It means we respect each other's boundaries and if we ever trespass against our neighbor's boundaries, we make amends insofar as possible, restoring double for what we have taken or destroyed, so that there are no hard feelings.

Kindness means that if my brother or sister or my neighbor is in trouble, I help him or her. *Kindness* means I answer Cain's question, "Am I my brother's keeper?" with a resounding "yes." And when I ask myself, "Who is my neighbor?" I remember the parable of the Good Samaritan and remember that my neighbor may even be someone who comes from the other side of the world or the other side of the tracks and may look like my enemy.

Walking humbly means I walk with God remembering who I am and who God is, which means remembering that I am not smarter than God or more in control than God is.

Let's not kid ourselves. The rent on life is pretty high if it means doing justice, loving mercy and walking humbly. Just think what it would mean in your own life to make sure all your relationships were fair and to make amends to all those you have trespassed against. Think what it would mean to reach out just to people in your family and among your closest acquaintances who are in trouble and really help them — to say nothing of reaching out to people on the other side of the tracks or the other side of the world. Above all, think what it would cost to walk humbly — to give up control, or the illusion of control, over everything in your world.

Jesus looked at the men who surrounded him and knew in his heart that they had already damaged their souls considerably because they had tried to protect their positions of power by denying other people justice or kindness. Jesus knew that if they killed him, an innocent man, in order to protect themselves, their souls would die.

It hurts our souls everyday when we engage in injustice. Nearly 20 years ago, Ronald Sider asked a very simple question: "Why do bananas which come from another continent cost less than apples which come from a neighboring county or state?" [2] Twenty years later bananas still cost less than apples. Either the apple grower is getting an exorbitant price for apples, or somebody who helps bring bananas to market is getting robbed.

I like bananas, but I refuse to pay more than 49 cents per pound for them. I like apples and sometimes I'm willing to pay $1.19 per pound for good ones in the off-season. I'm afraid that if I had to pay a fair price for bananas and a lot of other things, I wouldn't be able to afford them. Maybe I would starve. I ought to be more afraid of what injustice is doing to my soul.

I see a world full of people who don't have enough to eat or any shelter. I know that I really have more than I need. Nevertheless, I am afraid to share. I am afraid I won't have enough for me. But what does it do to my soul to have too much when others do not have enough? Maybe I should be more afraid of my soul dying than of anything else.

I don't really like this sermon. I'm probably going to ignore it, even though I preached it. I'm going to be like those people walking on those slippery rocks in plain sight of that sign that says that they could get killed walking on the rocks. I'm going to be like the religious leaders who surrounded Jesus who refused to listen to the warning in his parable. I'm going to be like the tenants in the vineyard who refused to pay the rent, unless . . . unless I walk humbly with God.

In the Sermon on the Mount, Jesus tells us that people who are poor in spirit are happy because they will have the kingdom of heaven. It is impossible to think about what it would take to really be just and really be kind in this world without feeling poor in spirit. It is impossible to look at that poverty of spirit, that coldness of heart, that lack of love and care, that deadness of soul without mourning. It is impossible to mourn for our lost souls without becoming meek and desiring to learn a better way of life by walking with Christ. Happy are those who see the warning signs and know that they are poor in spirit, for that is when life begins.

1. "Slippery Slope in Yosemite" *New York Times Magazine*, September 9, 1994, p. 14.
2. Sider, Ronald, *Rich Christians in a Hungry World*, (Downers Grove, IL: Intervarsity Press, 1977) pp. 163-165.

Lectionary Preaching
After Pentecost

Virtually all pastors who make use of the sermons in this book will find their worship life and planning shaped by one of two lectionary series. Most mainline Protestant denominations, along with clergy of the Roman Catholic Church, have now approved — either for provisional or official use — the three-year Revised Common (Consensus) Lectionary. This family of denominations includes United Methodist, Presbyterian, United Church of Christ and Disciples of Christ.

Lutherans and Roman Catholics, while testing the Revised Common Lectionary on a limited basis at present, follow their own three-year cycle of texts. While there are divergences between the Revised Common and Lutheran/Roman Catholic systems, the gospel texts show striking parallels, with few text selections evidencing significant differences. Nearly all the gospel texts included in this book will, therefore, be applicable to worship and preaching planning for clergy following either lectionary.

A significant divergence does occur, however, in the method by which specific gospel texts are assigned to specific calendar days. The Revised Common and Roman Catholic Lectionaries accomplish this by counting backwards from Christ the King (Last Sunday after Pentecost), discarding "extra" texts from the front of the list: Lutherans follow the opposite pattern, counting forward from The Holy Trinity, discarding "extra" texts at the end of the list.

The following index will aid the user of this book in matching the correct text to the correct Sunday during the Pentecost portion of the church year.

(Fixed dates do not pertain to Lutheran Lectionary)

Fixed Date Lectionaries *Revised Common and Roman Catholic*	Lutheran Lectionary *Lutheran*
The Day of Pentecost	The Day of Pentecost
The Holy Trinity	The Holy Trinity
May 29-June 4 — Proper 4, Ordinary Time 9	Pentecost 2
June 5-11 — Proper 5, Ordinary Time 10	Pentecost 3
June 12-18 — Proper 6, Ordinary Time 11	Pentecost 4
June 19-25 — Proper 7, Ordinary Time 12	Pentecost 5
June 26-July 2 — Proper 8, Ordinary Time 13	Pentecost 6

July 3-9 — Proper 9, Ordinary Time 14	Pentecost 7
July 10-16 — Proper 10, Ordinary Time 15	Pentecost 8
July 17-23 — Proper 11, Ordinary Time 16	Pentecost 9
July 24-30 — Proper 12, Ordinary Time 17	Pentecost 10
July 31-Aug. 6 — Proper 13, Ordinary Time 18	Pentecost 11
Aug. 7-13 — Proper 14, Ordinary Time 19	Pentecost 12
Aug. 14-20 — Proper 15, Ordinary Time 20	Pentecost 13
Aug. 21-27 — Proper 16, Ordinary Time 21	Pentecost 14
Aug. 28-Sept. 3 — Proper 17, Ordinary Time 22	Pentecost 15
Sept. 4-10 — Proper 18, Ordinary Time 23	Pentecost 16
Sept. 11-17 — Proper 19, Ordinary Time 24	Pentecost 17
Sept. 18-24 — Proper 20, Ordinary Time 25	Pentecost 18
Sept. 25-Oct. 1 — Proper 21, Ordinary Time 26	Pentecost 19
Oct. 2-8 — Proper 22, Ordinary Time 27	Pentecost 20
Oct. 9-15 — Proper 23, Ordinary Time 28	Pentecost 21
Oct. 16-22 — Proper 24, Ordinary Time 29	Pentecost 22
Oct. 23-29 — Proper 25, Ordinary Time 30	Pentecost 23
Oct. 30-Nov. 5 — Proper 26, Ordinary Time 31	Pentecost 24
Nov. 6-12 — Proper 27, Ordinary Time 32	Pentecost 25
Nov. 13-19 — Proper 28, Ordinary Time 33	Pentecost 26
	Pentecost 27
Nov. 20-26 — Christ the King	Christ the King

Reformation Day (or last Sunday in October) is October 31 (Revised Common, Lutheran)

All Saints' Day (or first Sunday in November) is November 1 (Revised Common, Lutheran, Roman Catholic)

Books In This Cycle A Series

Gospel Set
God In Flesh Made Manifest
Sermons For Advent, Christmas And Epiphany
Mark Radecke

Whispering The Lyrics
Sermons For Lent And Easter
Thomas Long

Christ Our Sure Foundation
Sermons For Pentecost (First Third)
Marc Kolden

Good News For The Hard Of Hearing
Sermons For Pentecost (Middle Third)
Roger G. Talbott

Invitations To The Light
Sermons For Pentecost (Last Third)
Phyllis Faaborg Wolkenhauer

First Lesson Set
Hope Beneath The Surface
Sermons For Advent, Christmas And Epiphany
Paul E. Robinson

Caught In The Acts
Sermons For Lent And Easter
Ed Whetstone

Tenders Of The Sacred Fire
Sermons For Pentecost (First Third)
Robert Cueni

What Do You Say To A Burning Bush?
Sermons For Pentecost (Middle Third)
Steven E. Burt

Veiled Glimpses Of God's Glory
Sermons For Pentecost (Last Third)
Robert S. Crilley

Second Lesson Set
Empowered By The Light
Sermons For Advent, Christmas And Epiphany
Richard A. Hasler

Ambassadors Of Hope
Sermons For Lent And Easter
Sandra Hefter Herrmann